The Basic Processes of Criminal Justice

GLENCOE PRESS CRIMINAL JUSTICE SERIES

Bloomquist: **Marijuana: The Second Trip**

Brandstatter/Hyman: **Fundamentals of Law Enforcement**

Brandstatter/Radelet: **Police and Community Relations**

Eldefonso: **Readings in Criminal Justice**

Gourley: **Effective Municipal Police Organization**

Koga/Nelson: **The Koga Method: Police Weaponless Control and Defense Techniques**

Koga/Nelson: **The Koga Method: Police Baton Techniques**

LeGrande: **The Basic Processes of Criminal Justice**

McArthur: **Police Patrol Pointers**

Melnicoe/Mennig: **Elements of Police Supervision**

Nelson: **Preliminary Investigation and Police Reporting: A Complete Guide to Police Written Communication**

Radelet: **The Police and the Community**

Radelet: **The Police and the Community: Studies**

Roberts/Bristow: **An Introduction to Modern Police Firearms**

Williams: **Narcotics and Drug Dependence**

General Editor:

G. DOUGLAS GOURLEY

Inspector (Ret.), LA Police Department
Chairman, Department of Criminal Justice
California State University at Los Angeles
Los Angeles, California

The Basic Processes of Criminal Justice

James L. LeGrande

Florida International University

GLENCOE PRESS
A division of Benziger Bruce & Glencoe, Inc.
Beverly Hills
Collier Macmillan Publishers
London

Printed in the United States of America

GLENCOE PRESS

A division of Benziger Bruce & Glencoe, Inc.

8701 Wilshire Boulevard

Beverly Hills, California 90211

Collier-Macmillan Canada, Ltd., Toronto, Canada

Library of Congress Catalog Card Number 72-85759

First printing, 1973

Dedicated to
Frank Russell LeGrande

The administration of justice is not an exact science. Its subject matter encompasses very nearly the totality of human experience, and is concentrated upon that area of life least subject to mathematical precision: relationships among persons. Furthermore, the administration of justice is a personal venture; no machine has yet been devised that can do justice, and none seems likely in the near future.

—Federal Judge Irving R. Kaufman

CONTENTS

PREFACE

The last decade has produced radical changes in the administration of criminal law. In 1961, the United States Supreme Court revolutionized the law of search and seizure after a police raiding party, which sought a bombing suspect in Cleveland, promiscuously searched a private home and discovered alleged pornography in a basement storage trunk. In 1963, the Court, in response to a handwritten petition by an aged Florida convict with a checkered career of crime, reversed long-standing precedent and required the state to appoint counsel for all indigent defendants charged with serious crimes. In 1964 and 1966, the Court upset traditional police methods of obtaining confessions by insisting that all Constitutional requirements be met to overcome the inherently coercive atmosphere of the interrogation room. Every critical stage of the criminal justice process has in some manner been significantly affected and altered during the past ten years as traditionally accepted practices have been closely scrutinized in the light of expanding concepts of due process.

During this same period of time civil disorders have increased, violence has erupted, and "law and order" has become a major political issue from the local ward to the White House. Presidential commissions have studied law enforcement and the administration of justice, the causes and prevention of violence, the effects of obscenity and pornography, and similar problems. Congress has passed "safe streets" acts and omnibus crime bills which appropriate millions of dollars for the improvement of criminal justice through hardware, technology, training and research. Spurred by the availability of funds, university and college campuses have introduced programs of training and education and launched research studies. States have appointed planning commissions to receive funds and devise means of implementing innovations. Bar associations and other legal groups have abandoned their previous stance of treating the criminal law as an undesirable stepchild and have conducted revealing studies into the nature of criminal justice.

Under these conditions, literature about criminal justice has expanded enormously. These publications may be classified into a number of categories. To meet the immediate needs of flourishing junior college and four-year programs in law enforcement, corrections, and criminal justice, many authors have rushed into print with basic introductory texts. These books for the most part have a tendency to oversimplify the operation of a complex system. Critical procedural steps or important policy processes are totally ignored or given a cursory examination. A second type of publication which has appeared is the technical piece which concerns itself with an in-depth examination of a technological problem, such as a special system for classifying ear prints, the use of helicopters for traffic control, or of voice prints for identification. Another category of books is philosophically oriented and concerned with the nature and purpose of criminal law, the role of the police in a democratic society, and similar concepts. Some books have been designed for use by law schools, and contain the text of judicial decisions frequently relating to highly technical legal aspects. And, finally, there is the highly sophisticated research publication which reports a well-documented, methodologically sound study of the variables involved in a police decision to arrest, the elements and factors that are involved in plea bargaining, and similar processes.

All of these resources provide beneficial services in one form or another but, unfortunately, place the student of criminal justice in a position of accepting an incomplete outline of the entire system or comprehensive treatment of a specialized portion only. The conscientious student, by undertaking laborious reading assignments, can, of course, overcome these shortcomings and obtain a relatively meaningful understanding of the administration of criminal law.

I have added this book to the growing list of criminal justice materials in an effort to strike a balance between these extremes. While attempting to avoid the pedantic, I have striven to include sufficient detail to enable the reader to acquire a basic knowledge of the processes involved. The reader interested in exploring specific topics further should find the bibliography a fertile field for detailed study.

Above all else, I have attempted to portray criminal justice as a human system. Criminal law is not impassionately formulated, objectively enforced, nor administered fully and strictly. It is a system of laws *and* men. Laws themselves are sterile and inanimate. Men give viability. The end result in any criminal case depends not so much on the organic structure of the substantive or procedural criminal law, as it does upon the exercise of discretion throughout the process. Ultimately the quality of criminal justice depends upon the caliber of the individuals who formulate policy and exercise discretion.

The Basic Processes of Criminal Justice

Chapter One

The Sources of Criminal Law

Criminal law had its beginning in antiquity. Our criminal law contains legacies from the Roman, Greek, and Germanic legal systems but it developed primarily in England following the Norman Conquest of 1066. English judges, functioning under a monarchy without a legislature, formalized the customs and practices of the people, executed and interpreted royal edicts, and applied the modicum of law inherited from previous ages. The decisions of these early judges were recorded, and a highly structured, formalized system of judge-made law evolved, following the doctrine of *stare decisis* whereby earlier decisions were considered binding precedent. This system is known as the *"common law."* In later years, when Parliament was created and legislation appeared in England for the first time, rather than replacing common law, the legislation was simply integrated into it, thus providing a consistent, viable system of criminal law.

The American colonies were controlled by the common law of England and such other special provisions that emanated from Parliament or the Crown. When the colonies obtained independence and became states, the police power was long in existence. *"Police power"*—the power to regulate persons and property within the jurisdiction for public health, safety, welfare, and morals, the power to establish criminal laws—was considered therefore, an inherent right of the state. As such, the state legislature possessed the right to alter, amend, or abrogate the common law.

The states delegated certain of their sovereign powers to the central federal government when they ratified the Constitution. The federal government is a limited government. It possesses no inherent power, not even that of generally controlling crime. It can designate crimes only in those areas in which the Constitution grants authority.

For administrative purposes, the states created certain governmental subunits (counties, townships, municipalities, villages, etc.) by constitution, statute, or charter. Depending upon the particular state's provisions, the subunits were granted a limited amount of authority to pass ordinances which made certain acts minor crimes. Through this means, the state further delegated portions of its police power.

Thus, historically and legally the legislature has acquired a number of responsibilities and powers:

1. The power to define acts or omissions that constitute crimes and to provide punishment for offenders.
2. The power to establish police agencies and to prescribe their duties and authority, including the power to organize and control such agencies.
3. The power to prescribe the procedural means of processing the offender through the adjudicatory and correctional processes.

On first examination, these powers may seem extremely broad. The legislature, however, is limited and controlled in the exercise of these powers by the relevant provisions of both the state and federal constitutions to assure that their enactments conform to the standards of due process of law.

The Concept of Crime

To define the word "crime" satisfactorily for all those with interest in this subject is a virtually impossible task. The search for an optimum definition leads the scholar through historical mazes, confusing legal distinctions, contradictory psychological and sociological theories, diverse political interpretations, conflicting theological dogma, and unending social philosophies. Jerome Frank, an eminent legal scholar, after previously defining the word "law" in a highly recognized treatise, subsequently conceded that he had seriously blundered in the attempt. After being assailed by other law definers, he conceded that such undertakings were futile, time-consuming contests, amounting to "silly word battles."[1]

However, by viewing "crime" in a strict legal context and by divorcing it from any consideration of philosophical, moral, or social concepts, a reasonable working definition can be formulated. This type of definition can be challenged as abstract and sterile but, regardless of its shortcomings, it offers a highly pragmatic alternative to Frank's "silly word battles," and provides a sound first step for an elementary examination of the system of criminal justice. With these qualifications, the following paragraphs describe a legal concept of crime.

Crime is a wrong against public interests to which a governmental jurisdiction has attached a penalty. It is an act which has been committed, or omitted, in violation of a public law either prohibiting or commanding it.

The law may prohibit the commission of overt acts such as robbery, rape, burglary, speeding, or disorderly conduct. It may also require that acts be done so that an individual's failure to act may constitute a violation of the criminal law. Failure to file an income tax return, failure to maintain adequate health standards where food is dispensed for public consumption, and failure to dispose of garbage properly are examples of crimes based upon an individual's failure to act.

The legal action against one committing a crime is brought in the name of the governmental jurisdiction. The commission of a criminal act is not a private matter between the criminal and his victim; rather it is considered an offense against the peace and dignity of the governmental jurisdiction. The victim has no inherent right to initiate a criminal action against the offender. The prerogative and discretion of initiating criminal proceedings rests with the government and its agencies. Any damages recovered in the form of fines, costs, or imprisonment are deemed to be the property of the government.

One act may give rise to both a criminal and a civil cause of action. As an example, Jones maliciously sets fire to Smith's home. Smith may bring a civil action against Jones to recover the damage to his property, and the state may file criminal charges against Jones for arson. For practical purposes, these cases are handled independently, neither relating to the other.

Crime is classified by grades, generally in accordance with the degree of penalty attached. The three usual classifications of crimes are treason, felony, and misdemeanor. Treason consists of levying war or giving aid or comfort to the enemy. A felony is a crime which has been so designated by the legislative unit, or which carries a penalty of death or imprisonment in a state prison. Misdemeanors are crimes so designated by the legislative unit, or which carry a penalty of less than one year, to be served in an institution other than a state prison, such as a city or county jail. Although the foregoing represents the generally accepted rules, some jurisdictions may vary from these rules and prescribe prison sentence for misdemeanors or less than one year confinement for felonies. The distinction between grades of crime becomes highly important in relation to the power of arrest, the amount of force permissible in making an arrest, the judicial forum of the trial, and related areas of criminal procedure. The legislative branch of government has the power to establish, define, and provide the degree of punishment for crimes.

Enactment of Criminal Statutes

The legislature may declare an act to be a crime, even though previously the act was perfectly legal. Such legislation, however, cannot be retroactive.

In the enactment of a criminal statute the legislature may define the crime by (1) giving it a name which existed at common law without further definition, (2) specifically define the acts or omission involved, or (3) define the results that the act is calculated to produce without describing the means utilized. Regardless of the method of definition, the statute must convey to a person of ordinary intelligence an adequate description of the prohibited or required conduct. Failure to meet this requirement of clarity normally results in the statute being declared invalid because of uncertainty.

The legislature may define the degree, class, or grade of a crime. It may classify the crime as a misdemeanor or a felony at its discretion. Because of the legislative discretion, it is not unusual to find the commission of the same act in different states may carry grossly diverse punishment. For example, in most states shoplifting a ten-cent candy bar from a business establishment is a misdemeanor. However, in Michigan a statute describes larceny from a building as a felony; thus, shoplifting a ten-cent item can be prosecuted as a felony in Michigan.

Because of the various levels of our government, one act may constitute a breach of the criminal law of two or more sovereignties. Based on this concurrent jurisdiction more than criminal prosecution may result. The robbery of a national bank constitutes a crime against both federal and state laws. An individual who steals an automobile in Wichita, Kansas, and drives one hundred miles to Enid, Oklahoma, has offended the laws of three jurisdictions. He may be tried for (1) car theft in Kansas, (2) transporting stolen property in Oklahoma, and (3) transporting stolen property between states in a federal court.

In order to be valid, a criminal statute must prescribe the penalty for the commission of prohibited conduct. The penalty may be prescribed in the specific statute which designated the crime or it may be provided in a separate statute. The statute designating the crime may simply specify that it is a misdemeanor or a felony. A separate general statute may prescribe the punishment for all misdemeanors or felonies not otherwise specified. This statute will be held valid. Some state courts have avoided this requirement by holding that when no punishment is prescribed for a particular crime, the offense may be punished by the assessment of a fine only. The amount of punishment prescribed for a specific offense is generally considered a matter wholly within the power and discretion of the legislature, so long as no constitutional provisions are violated.

As a corollary to the legislature's power to create, it has the power to destroy. The legislature at its discretion may amend or repeal an existing criminal law. Unless the legislature provides to the contrary, no prosecution may be undertaken for a violation of the statute that occurred prior to its repeal. This concept is based on the theory that the repeal constituted a form of "legislature pardon" for past acts. When the legislature attaches a "saving clause" to the repealing statute, violations occurring prior to the repeal may be brought to final judgment. Some states have automatic saving clauses in their constitutions. In these states, the prosecution of cases prior to repeal is outside legislative determination.

The general philosophy of the criminal law is that there should be no punishment unless the accused intended to commit the act or unless the accused engaged in conduct of such gross negligence that it may be construed as an intent. Despite this general philosophy of not punishing the "innocent mind," the legislature may forbid the commission of an act without regard to the intent or knowledge of the doer. This power, of course, is qualified by reasonableness, in that the legislature could not establish as a crime an act that could not be avoided regardless of the amount of care and circumspection that a person utilized. Normally, such "absolute liability" crimes are regulatory in nature, deal with minor offenses, and involve elements of public necessity and practicality. For example, an individual drives a motor vehicle at the speed of fifty miles per hour in a thirty-five mile per hour zone; it is virtually impossible to prove intent in this type of case. Further, the legislature has deemed it necessary to public safety that speed be controlled. Thus, legislatures do not require an intent in speeding cases.

Motive, or the reason why the crime was committed, is not an essential or necessary element of a crime. Regardless of an individual's laudable or altruistic rationale, the strict letter of the statutory law does not require its consideration. As a practical matter, motive may become highly relevant in the trial of the case and there is little doubt that many defendants have been given freedom for high-minded reasons or because the state has failed to prove a malevolent motive.

In many states, the common law of crimes has been specifically repealed by statute, abrogated by implication either through adoption of a criminal law that embraces the total basic subject matter, or through enactment of statutes that are clearly inconsistent with common law. Nonetheless, even where it has officially been abolished by statute, common law still has a profound effect upon criminal law. If a state statute defines a crime by the use of a common law term, e.g., burglary, robbery, embezzlement, etc., but fails to define the elements or series of acts which constitute that crime, the courts will rely upon the common law definition in the trial and review of the case. The common law is used as a point of reference or definition even when the legislature defines the crime. In defining the crime of burglary, the legislature may use the term "breaking." The courts in turn may use the common law definition of "breaking" in interpreting the statute.

While recognizing that (1) the ever-present specter of the common law exerts a great influence on the criminal law, (2) the judiciary possesses an overriding power through utilization of constitutional interpretation, and (3) criminal activity of certain limited nature is outside the sphere of legislative action, it can be concluded for practical purposes that the legislature has the sole responsibility and prerogative for establishing crimes and punishments. In the final analysis crime is what the legislature declares it to be.

Discussion Questions

1. Critics of the judicial system charge that some judges are making new law instead of interpreting the constitution and legislative enactments. Discuss this criticism within the historical context of the common law.
2. What are the consequences of adhering to a strict application of the doctrine of *stare decisis* in a complex society? What are the consequences of totally abandoning such a doctrine?
3. Numerous candidates for federal political offices have raised "crime in the streets" and "law and order" as national issues. Given the facts that the primary police power resides in the states and the federal government does not possess inherent powers, how may these candidates fulfill their promises to have an impact on local crime?
4. In many criminal cases, the state is required to prove criminal intent in order to obtain convictions, but motive is not an essential element. What is the distinction between intent and motive? What implications does this distinction have for individuals engaged in nonviolent civil disobedience to protest what they consider adverse social conditions?

Chapter Two

The Effective Limits of Criminal Law

In exercising the state's police power, the legislature has attempted to utilize the criminal law to accomplish many different and diverse purposes.

Although there are many different philosophies concerning the purpose of the criminal law, most authorities concede that its prime purpose is the protection of life and property from vicious or aggressive attack. This concept of security of the person and the right of enjoyment of personal property appears to be the fundamental basis of criminal law. Throughout this country, legislatures have provided severe penalties for murder, aggravated assault, rape, robbery, burglary, and theft. Such crimes of aggression on person or property are considered *mala in se*—immoral or wrong by their very nature.

A second category of crimes, which constitutes a large portion of the criminal law, can be best described as *regulatory*. Regulatory laws are designed to provide a degree of conformity for the purposes of safety, efficiency, and convenience. Perhaps the best example of this is the thousands of traffic laws in this country. There is no question of morality involved in a legislative policy decision as to whether automobiles should be driven on the right or left side of a highway. Such laws are not concerned with eradicating "evil," but with providing a uniform system so that each citizen has a reasonable basis for predicting others' driving habits and is thus assured greater safety, less congestion, and more convenience. These crimes are *mala prohibita*—bad only because the legislature has prohibited such action. No moral turpitude is involved.

A third group of crimes contains elements of a regulatory nature while also being concerned with promoting honesty and morality. These laws prohibit such acts as the sale of impure foods and drugs, filing inaccurate asset statements with security exchange commissions, pollution of the environment with industrial wastes, obtaining property under false pretenses, and similar offenses. These acts are dishonest in that they deceitfully acquire another's property or deliberately misrepresent a product or heedlessly damage public domain for profit. But the aim of these laws is not so much concerned with the alteration of human character traits and maintaining high moral standards as it is with protecting other individuals or the community in general. As opposed to the *mala in se* and *regulatory* groupings, these offenses can be classified as *protective crimes*.

A fourth category of crimes arises from the attempt to regulate personal morality. Such crimes are traditionally referred to as *vice crimes* and include such offenses as fornication, adultery, illicit cohabitation, abortion, sodomy, homosexual acts, prostitution, and pornography. In most situations these offenses occur in private between consenting adults. This characteristic is what distinguishes them as crimes involving personal morality, since the elements of the *mala in se, regulatory,* and *protective* categories are generally not present.

A final category of crime involves the use of narcotics and alcohol. Although these activities are frequently considered vice offenses, there are additional characteristics which distinguish them. In most vice crimes, the participants retain the ability to terminate the activity. The addict and the alcoholic, however, are psychologically and physiologically dependent and can seldom voluntarily terminate their continuous offenses. When dealing with the addict or the chronic alcoholic, the question of morality becomes a *medical problem*—and, considering the widespread ramification, a *social problem*.

One might devise different or additional groupings of the type of problems that the legislature attempts to remedy with the criminal law. Certain types of crimes may overlap into more than one group. However, the foregoing does illustrate that the criminal law has no single purpose and that it has been utilized in an attempt to correct many varieties of social ills.

Since crime is basically what the legislature defines it to be, millions of criminals can be created by one legislative enactment. In theory, basing its action upon the scientific evidence that "cigarette smoking may be hazardous to your health," a state legislature could pass a law prohibiting the manufacture, possession, sale, or use of cigarettes. Many other presently legitimate activities could be "criminalized" by utilizing the police power of the state. Thus, crime cannot be characterized as a natural state of evil or depravity.

The legislature, functioning as a policy maker, has a tremendous responsibility in determining whether or not the criminal sanction should be applied. It is not a decision to be considered lightly, but one which should be undertaken only after a thorough examination of all relevant circumstances, possible reactions, and other alternatives.

Practical lawmaking requires the legislature to have a well-developed knowledge of the nature, customs, and traditions of those individuals who are to be affected by the law. It requires an understanding of the degree of efficiency, the availability of resources, and the competence of those responsible for the law's enforcement and administration. The legislature should be cognizant of the practical problems involved, such as the necessary enforcement techniques, procedural restraints, and community reactions. The legislature should seek data from other jurisdictions, review historical implications, avail itself of recognized experts in the field, and seek every source of information pertaining to the practical effect of the proposed legislation.

Frequently, new legislation is enacted—or old laws retained—without full consideration of their true impact, their enforceability, or the practical problems that they might create. In terms of desired effect it is normally presumed that a vast majority of the population will take notice of a law and voluntarily conform; another segment will not voluntarily conform but will respond because of a coercive fear of being prosecuted or will be deterred because of visible or threatened enforcement action; and a third much smaller group will become the target of enforcement action and ultimately will receive punishment and/or correction.

While these presumptions may be true in many cases, there is a tendency for legislatures and much of the public to overestimate the influence of the criminal law on behavior. At this stage of our societal development, where the offense causes substantive harm to persons, property, economic interests, or public safety generally, the criminal law is clearly accepted as one necessary remedy. The criminal law in this country, however, has been expanded far beyond these fundamental offenses and includes many highly intangible ones.

Experience has indicated that the criminal law is an extremely ineffective tool for imposing moral standards of conduct on the populace. It is also ill equipped to cope with medical problems and general social problems. Unfortunately, in many instances, legislation has placed this responsibility upon the police. The examination of a few examples follows.

Drunkenness: The police agencies in this country annually make approximately two million arrests for the offense of public drunkenness. This great volume of inebriates constitutes one of every three arrests made in America. In those few jurisdictions which do not have specific laws relating to drunkenness, the individual is arrested for disorderly conduct, vagrancy, loitering, or similar offenses. The various laws provide maximum penalties from five days to six months. In some states, statutes provide for two years' imprisonment for being habitually drunk. The clientele range from the first-time offender to the chronic alcoholic. There is strong evidence that a large number of the arrestees have lengthy drunkenness arrest records and that a disproportionate number are poor people who live in the slums.[1]

In its extensive study of drunkenness the President's Crime Commission found:

- After arrest the drunk is usually placed in a barren tank cell for a few hours.
- The chronic offender generally suffers from a variety of ailments, deaths occasionally occur in the tank, but medical care is rarely provided there.
- Usually the offender has no money for bail and appears in court with a group of fifteen or twenty others, with few due process safeguards during trial.
- During a hasty hearing, the defendant is usually released or sentenced to several days in jail.
- During his sentence, he is sheltered and fed at state expense.
- After serving the sentence he is released, still without financial resources or employment, and often is rearrested in a matter of days or hours to begin the cycle again.[2]

The President's Crime Commission concluded:

> The criminal justice system appears ineffective to deter drunkenness or to meet the problems of the chronic alcoholic offender. What the system does accomplish is to remove the drunk from public view, detoxify him, and provide him with food, shelter, emergency medical service, and a brief period of forced sobriety. As presently constituted, the system is not in a position to meet his underlying medical and social problems. . . . Drunkenness should not itself be a criminal offense.[3]

When one considers that one-third of the arrests made by police officers in this country are for drunkenness; that since it is a criminal offense, the drunk must be processed through the courts (regardless of how hastily); and that a vast majority of short-term confinements in jails are for this offense, the tremendous burden placed on the criminal justice system by this problem becomes evident. The expenditure of these resources would be worthwhile if the problem were corrected, but to the chronic alcoholic the process becomes little more than a merry-go-round life style. One source has conservatively estimated the annual expenditure for handling drunkenness offenders at $100 million.[4]

Although at this point no totally effective treatment of alcoholism is known, alternatives to the criminal process are available. It should be recognized that drunkenness is a medical and social problem, not a crime problem. Public health personnel or other nonpolice public servicemen could be used to process drunks; civil detoxification centers —like the one in St. Louis—could be established, staffed by trained medical personnel; public health after-care programs could be developed, including housing, employment, and other needs; private resources and voluntary social agencies could be utilized where possible; and police coordination could be established for apprehension and referral, when necessary. There are over five million alcoholics in the country. Alcoholism is considered the nation's third largest public health problem. So long as the alcoholic continues his cyclic rounds through the police paddy wagon, the courtroom, and the jail, no solution will be reached. So long as he is treated as a criminal, this pathetic situation will continue.

Abortion: While several states have begun total reform or liberalization of their abortion laws in recent years, most states rely on criminal statutes patterned after an English law of 1803, which was adopted when medicine lacked its present skill and technology.

Laws against abortion are highly unenforceable. Convictions for this crime are exceedingly low. Many law enforcement officers believe the abortionist is performing a useful service. No doubt the officers are reflecting the public's attitude about the enforcement of this law. Since it is estimated that illegal abortions exceed one million annually,[5] considerable doubt may be raised as to whether the criminal law truly reflects community standards and beliefs. The fact that 34,175 women received legal abortions in New York during the first four months after the state's new liberalized abortion statute became effective casts further light on public attitudes.[6]

Even when abortion was universally illegal in this country, the upper and middle classes had little difficulty obtaining abortions in clinic or hospital-type surroundings with competent personnel, while members of the lower socioeconomic classes were forced to resort to similar operations in kitchens and back rooms with personnel of questionable competence. What is medically considered a simple and safe operation under proper conditions was converted by the law to a degrading and sometimes dangerous practice for those of the lower economic class. Today, with legal abortions available a few hours away by airplane, those states that retain strict abortion laws grossly increase this discrimination.

Abortion law, then, (1) does not accurately reflect community standards; (2) is virtually unenforceable because of the nature of the transaction; (3) gives rise to illicit abortionists who earn large fees; and (4) is highly discriminatory to the lower socioeconomic class.

While opinions on the morality of having an abortion differ significantly, millions of women continue to obtain this illegal operation. It is certainly appropriate to reexamine the abortion laws realistically to determine both the appropriateness and effectiveness of the criminal sanction.

Sexual Offenses: Legislation in virtually every state prohibits extramarital intercourse, homosexual acts, and "abnormal" sexual activities between man and woman (even husband and wife). The message from the legislature is clear: private sexual activity is to be restricted to those in legal matrimony and is to follow "normal" methodology. One might question whether this is a meaningful community standard when one considers research findings that 95 percent of the population have violated these laws.[7] Another major consideration is enforceability. Short of equipping every prospective copulation area with closed circuit television, the enforcement task is virtually impossible.

The criminal law unquestionably has a role to play in protecting naive children from sexually mature adults, in suppressing solicitation or sexual activity in public, and in intervening when sexual advantage is obtained by force or fraud. But where the activity occurs between consenting adults in private, the legislatures should take the necessary steps to abolish the law.

The Criminal Law May Stimulate Additional Crime

The passage or retention of legislation may substantially contribute to the formation of an even larger crime problem. When the new legislation outlaws formerly legal activities, goods, or services, the purchasers must forsake their former practices or seek illegal sources of supply. In many cases, the latter is the usual course. The more effective that the police are in enforcing the law, the scarcer the product or service becomes and, consequently the higher the market price. This inflation provides illicit suppliers with the opportunity for high profits, some of which may be utilized for expansion of the operation and for bribery of police and other officials.

Experiences in crime control offer several examples where an attempt to control a problem by the enactment of a criminal statute not only miserably failed but greatly increased the severity of the problem that it sought to control. Probably one of the best instances was the Eighteenth Amendment which prohibited the manufacture, sale, transport, import, or export of alcoholic beverages for about thirteen years.

It is instructive to note the following preprohibition and prohibition data:

1. In the preprohibition era there were 15,000 saloons in New York —after liquor was declared contraband, there were 32,000 speakeasies.[8]
2. Before prohibition the annual per capita consumption of intoxicants was 1.84 gallons. During prohibition it was 1.95 gallons. In 1968 it was 1.7 gallons.[9]
3. Significant growth of the national crime syndicate occurred to meet the demands of the thirsty citizens. The prohibition era has been characterized as playing a tremendous role in the transformation of terroristic bands into efficiently organized criminal syndicates.

Many authorities indicate that similar conditions exist today because of criminal laws restricting certain types of activities and services. A recent economic analysis of organized crime indicates:

> . . . black-market crimes—gambling, dope, smuggling, etc.— . . . are absolutely dependent upon the law and on some degree of enforcement. That is, without a law that excludes legitimate competition, the basis for monopoly probably could not exist. . . . With virtually no enforcement, either because enforcement is not attempted or because enforcement is unfeasible, the black market could not be profitable enough to invite criminal monopoly. . . An important difference between black-market crimes and most others . . . is that they are "crimes" only because we have chosen to legislate against the commodify or service they provide . . . . It is a matter of policy that determines the black markets.[10]

The analysis further indicates that such legislation tends to create numerous costs to society. It gives the criminal the same type of protection that a tariff gives a domestic concern—a guarantee of the absence of competition from the legal businessman. It provides special incentive to corrupt the police, who themselves can assist in eliminating unwanted competition. The consumers, for the most part average citizens, are taught contempt for the law. It provides the criminal cartel with sufficient funds to maintain itself and infiltrate legitimate businesses.[11]

Approaching the problem from the economic point of view, the report predicts: "If narcotics were not illegal, there could be no black market and no monopoly profits, and the interest in 'pushing' it would probably be not much greater than the pharmaceutical interest in pills to reduce the symptoms of the common cold."[12]

Conclusion

There is more than ample evidence to illustrate that the criminal law is not an effective instrument to correct or eliminate social and health problems, such as drunkenness or narcotic addiction, or personal morality matters such as fornication, adultery, and homosexuality, and commercial vice activities such as gambling, prostitution, and loan sharking with consenting victims and consumers. Many of these laws are unenforceable and accomplish little more than breeding disrespect or contempt for the legal system. In other cases, such as abortion, the law is ineffective with the upper and middle classes, but serves as a discriminatory barrier to the lower socioeconomic classes attempting to obtain similar services. And finally, in some circumstances the criminal law serves to aggravate the problem by making it economically feasible for a criminal organization to provide the prohibited services and gain financial profits and inordinate influence.

This evidence, convincing as it is, does not necessarily mean that the legislature should immediately abolish the pertinent criminal laws and forget about the problems, nor does it mean that the police and other agencies of criminal justice should categorically label them as "social problems" to be processed by "social workers." It does mean that legislatures, police, courts, and others should seek alternative means, outside the criminal law, not only to handle, but to alleviate and correct the problem. Criminal law in these areas may provide a stop gap, but it is not a remedy.

Alcoholism is a public health problem, an illness, not a crime. It should be attacked by detoxification centers, counseling programs, after-care programs, and meaningful medical and psychiatric studies.

Abortion should be treated as a personal decision by the woman, in consultation with her family and her physician. Sexual activities of every kind and description between *consenting adults in private* should be outside the scope of criminal law.

Narcotic addiction is a medical problem and an illness. A system of treatment, coupled with prevention and educational programs and appropriate minimal supplementary criminal laws, should be established. A system, perhaps patterned after that employed in Britain, should be considered to eliminate the enormous profit from drug traffic.

When society demands that the criminal law assume the total burden of social control—the responsibilities of home, school, church, and other social institutions—along with various and sundry problems of medicine, morality, and manners, criminal justice agencies and functionaries become ineffective. This ineffectiveness develops from overambitious or oversimplistic plans of the legislature to regulate every phase of human endeavor, and/or the resort to criminal law to compensate for the deficiencies of other agencies of social control and social service. The use of the criminal law for *mala in se,* protective, and regulatory activities in most cases may be justified. Extension of criminal law beyond this point involves behavior that by its very nature does not lend itself to the criminal justice system's instrumentalities of external coercion.

Perhaps this excessive reliance is in part the result of the citizen's faith that the criminal law is an effective method (or an inexpensive way) of handling social problems. Perhaps some believe that moral duties and the laws of God should be transformed into legal duties. But such undertakings ultimately lead to a failure in enforcement, an aggravation of the problem, and a nullification of the legislature's avowed intent. Eventually this creates cynicism toward the law and its enforcement agencies and fosters indifference, apathy, and disrespect in the public.

After studying the need for reform in the substantive criminal law the President's Crime Commission commented: "Undoubtedly a great deal of research is needed on the uses and limitations of the criminal law as a means of social regulation. . . . But enough is now known to warrant abandonment of the common legislative premise that the criminal law is a sure panacea for all social ailments. . . ."[13]

There are no simple solutions to most social problems. The legislator has an awesome task in formulating policies. From the alternatives presented it is frequently easier to rely upon the less controversial "solution" of passing a criminal law than to become embroiled in innovative, untried programs. What is important is that other alternatives be considered and that the student of criminal justice does not become so discipline bound that he cannot seek the answer outside the realm of criminal law.

Discussion Questions

1. Assume that a state legislature passes a statute prohibiting the manufacture, possession, sale, and use of cigarettes within its jurisdictional boundaries. What events are likely to occur, and what impact would they have on the criminal justice system within the state?
2. Should the state legislature utilize the criminal law to regulate conduct which is related to personal morality?
3. Some observers of the political scene indicate that one reason legislatures are hesitant to act on abortion reform is the fear of political repercussions from the voters. If this be the case, would a state referendum of the question to the voters possibly resolve this issue? What are the advantages and disadvantages of such an undertaking?
4. Before passing a law should the legislature consider its enforceability as a crucial factor? What is the significance of having unenforceable laws in effect?

Chapter Three

The Establishment and Control of Police Agencies

Unless specifically restricted by the state constitution, the state legislature is vested with the authority to establish the law enforcement agencies that shall exist within the state, the duties that law enforcement officers will perform, and the authority that the officers may exercise in the performance of those duties.

The approaches taken to create law enforcement units have varied from state to state in relation to detail provisions, but a number of general patterns have emerged.

State Level Police Agencies

Every state except Hawaii has established enforcement units responsible to the governor. Such agencies include highway patrols, state police, alcoholic beverage control units, conservation divisions, organized crime bureaus, and various other special purpose organizations. More than two hundred state law enforcement units are in existence today. As creatures of statute, the officers of these agencies may perform only those duties and exercise only the authority granted. While some of these agencies have broad general authority, most are restricted to limited investigative or enforcement endeavors. Even when an agency is granted the authority to enforce all state laws, it generally avoids urban areas that maintain their own police forces.

The County Sheriff

Every state has a sheriff system operating at the county level of government. Most of the states have created this office by broad constitution provision, leaving the legislature the responsibility of imposing specific duties and defining the sheriff's authority. Legislatures tend to be very general in the assignment of such duties. As an example, the Illinois statutes provide that the sheriff will have the following responsibilities:

> . . . custody and care of the courthouse and jail . . . serve and execute . . . and return all writs, warrants, process, orders, and decree of every description that may be legally directed . . . to them . . . conservator of the peace . . . keep the same, suppress riots, routs, affrays, fighting, breeches of the peace, and prevent crime; . . . arrest offenders . . . attend upon all courts of record held in his county . . . and obey the lawful orders and directions of the court. . . . enforce all the laws . . . [and] ordinances . . . relating to the regulation of motor vehicle traffic and the promotion of safety on the public highways. . . . suppress all riots and unlawful assemblies, to keep the peace, and without delay to serve and execute all warrants, writs, precept, and other process to him lawful directed.[1]

Beyond the general duties enumerated above, the Illinois statutes place dozens of other responsibilities upon the sheriff. These include: appraisal of land acquired by the state at an execution sale, selling property under court order, transporting prisoners, conducting civil rights investigations, and assisting in enforcing the "Animal Disease Act."

With minor exception, the sheriff is an elected official. His term of office is usually limited either to two or to four years. It is not unusual to find a provision prohibiting the sheriff succeeding himself in office or one limiting his tenure to two terms. Normally the only qualifications that an individual must possess to seek the office of sheriff are age and residency. Although there are a few exceptions, in most jurisdictions the position is a prize bestowed by the electorate upon the most charismatic candidate of the dominant political party. With short tenure in office, political debts to repay, lack of expertise in criminal justice, and a public image to maintain, a sheriff's administrative and operational decisions frequently may be oriented more to public relations than to professional law enforcement services. There is a desperate need to reconstruct sheriff systems in most states to attract qualified personnel.

Municipal Police Departments

Today, when confronted with the problems of policing cities and urban areas, nearly all state legislatures have preferred to delegate their power to create police agencies to the municipal governments which then establish, organize, and administer their own police departments. Although the states have freely delegated this authority, they have maintained control over the amount of authority a municipal officer may exercise in performing his duties. Approximately 36,000 separate agencies exist today to police cities, towns, and villages.

When such delegation is made to the municipality, the city normally creates and regulates the police department by ordinance or charter provisions. Direct supervision and control of the department is usually vested in the mayor or the city manager, as the city's chief executive. He generally appoints the chief of police, who reports directly to him concerning police operations. The chief of police is generally subject to removal at the pleasure of the executive. Although this type of control structure exists in the vast majority of American cities, a number of cities utilize appointed police boards; control by the city council, commission or board; or election of the chief of police by the community.

State Control of Municipal Police

Even though the state possesses the power to control, organize, and administer municipal police departments itself, the practice is to delegate the actual organization and administration to local officials. There are some notable exceptions and they serve to illustrate the legislative power that lies dormant.

For example, according to Chapter 84 of the Missouri Statutes, the St. Louis Metropolitan Police Department is state controlled. The governor of the state appoints a four-man Board of Police Commissioners. The mayor of the city is an *ex officio* member of the board, without vote. The board has total control over the internal organization and administration of the department. State statute further provides for the number of personnel, their ranks, salaries, qualifications, and working hours. The city is prohibited by statute from passing ordinances conflicting or interfering with the power of the Board of Police Commissioners. The board annually prepares a budget for the operation of the department for the next year. It is certified to the city and the city is required to appropriate the specified amount, without contest. Under the operation of these statutes, the city or the citizens thereof have no direct legal means of interfering with the operations of the department.

Although the situation in St. Louis is unique, it illustrates the power of the state legislature.

Federal Agencies

By virtue of the Ninth and Tenth Amendments, the federal government has only those powers granted or delegated to it by the Constitution. By a well-established principle of constitutional interpretation, powers which were not expressly granted to the national government are reserved to the states. Since the general police power was not granted to the federal government, no centralized national police force with broad enforcement power may be established in the United States. National law enforcement agencies, however, can be legally justified by Article I, Section 8, Paragraph 18. This clause deals with "implied powers" of the Congress to facilitate implementation of its laws. Congress is given the power to pass appropriate legislation and to create a law-enforcement unit to assure sufficient enforcement power to the executive branch to carry the law into effect.

An example: Since Congress was granted constitutional authority (Article I, Section 8, Paragraph 6) to provide for punishment of counterfeiting the security and coin of the United States, the Secret Service, an agency possessing law enforcement power, was created as a necessary means of detecting and apprehending counterfeiters. Postal inspectors, custom officers, and FBI agents have legal justification based respectively upon congressional powers relating to post roads, imports, and interstate commerce. Federal agencies with law enforcement duties must depend upon the Constitution as the ultimate source of authority validating their existence, coupled with a federal statute defining their powers and duties.

Federal police have the broadest geographical jurisdiction possible —all states, territories, and possessions of the United States—while state and local officers under normal circumstances are limited to the boundaries of their respective entities. Federal police, however, have very limited subject matter jurisdiction. They possess authority to investigate and apprehend offenders of the federal law, which in turn is limited by the delegated constitutional authority. The Federal Bureau of Investigation, the national law-enforcement agency with the most generous jurisdiction, is limited to the enforcement of less than two hundred laws. State and local police may have the responsibility for enforcing literally thousands.

With the expansion of interstate movement of people and goods and the concern about insuring civil rights as well as the spread of organized crime and civil disturbances, federal involvement in areas previously considered state responsibility has significantly increased in recent years. In most of these situations, the federal government is acquiring jurisdiction to punish offenders under federal laws, when similar statutes already exist at the state level. The purpose of such legislation appears to be to provide a means of avoiding fragmented investigations by local units and to insure an integrated, well-coordinated handling of the case. Thus far, there has been only limited objection to this approach. Continued extension of this practice, however, might well lead to federal policymaking in areas historically reserved to the states.

Conclusion

The legislative units of government on the federal, state, and local levels possess in various degrees the power to create, regulate, organize, administer, control, and supervise law enforcement units in the United States. Police agencies obtain their very existence, and police officers their authority and power, through statutory provisions. The legislature is the first vital link in the chain of agencies involved in the administration of criminal justice. Its responsibility is to provide the basic administrative framework and the necessary authority for the police to operate efficiently, while simultaneously providing sufficient control to avoid excessive police power and the abuse of individual rights.

There is some indication that in the future legislatures may assume a more active role in this area. Some legislatures have established mandatory minimum training requirements for all police officers in the state. Others are considering the establishment of minimum qualifications for employment, minimum salary standards, and similar means of obtaining higher quality candidates. Should the legislatures choose to do so, they are in a unique position to upgrade law enforcement significantly through their authority to establish and control police agencies.

Discussion Questions

1. What steps could a state legislature take to improve the quality of the sheriff system within the state?
2. In many urbanized areas there are a dozen or more police agencies with adjacent jurisdictional boundaries. Each agency is autonomous and has its own administrative and logistical support. What results might occur if the state legislature, for law enforcement purposes, consolidated these jurisdictions and formed a state level metropolitan police force?
3. Would it be feasible for the state, through appropriate legislation or, if necessary, constitutional amendment, to administer *all* law enforcement activities within its boundaries?
4. Should the state legislature establish qualifications for employment, standards for training, salary levels, and similar controls over all police officers in the state? The advantages are obvious, but what are the disadvantages?

Chapter Four

The Authority to Arrest

The authority to arrest was not originally established by statute, but evolved from the custom and practices of common law dating back at least to the twelfth century. By the end of the sixteenth century the laws of arrest were formalized and highly structured. The basic principles have undergone very few significant changes since that time. Today, each state has its own constitutional provisions, statutes, and judicial decisions regulating the exercise of arrest powers. Some have substantially retained the common law provisions, while most have slightly expanded the police officer's authority and adopted provisions discouraging citizens from making arrests. There are variations in the arrest laws between jurisdictions, but when the minor technical aspects are discounted, a common philosophical and practical pattern emerges. The purpose of this chapter is to examine these common characteristics.

Operationally defined, arrest means taking a person into physical custody for the alleged commission of a crime in order to initiate a criminal action in a court of competent jurisdiction. The term "arrest" is extremely amorphous. Judge Irving R. Kaufman made the following observations in *United States* v. *Bonanno*:[1]

> It is axiomatic that before a finding can be made that there has been an illegal arrest, a showing must be made that there has been an arrest. Thus, an immediate problem of definition arises. Joined to that problem is the danger, that the defining process will cast an air of deceptive simplicity over the broader task actually faced by the Court. One

> must never forget that this is a decision on the rights of individuals and the duty of government, and not an abstract exercise in definition. In dealing with words there is always a temptation to allow them to become separated from this objective correlative in the everyday world, and to treat them as if they have, or ought to have, one single simple meaning, unaffected by the context in which they occur and divorced from the world of things and events which give them their content and justification. "Arrest" is just such a word, not only because it is necessarily unspecific and descriptive of complex, often extended processes, but because in different contexts it describes different processes, each of which has built up, in both legal and common parlance, sharply divergent emotional connotations.

The general elements or requisites of an arrest by a police officer are:

1. There must be an intent on the part of the officer to make an arrest; an intent to deprive the individual of his liberty and freedom of action; and an intent to restrain him physically if he does not peacefully submit.
2. The officer must inform the individual of his intention to place him under arrest, and the reason or cause for the arrest.
3. The officer must identify the authority under which he acts. If the officer is clearly uniformed this requirement is normally met.
4. The individual must be placed under the officer's actual control. If the officer communicates his intention, authority, and reason for the arrest, and the individual submits to the officer and obeys his commands, an arrest is made. Although, technically, no touching or subduing is required, most legal authorities recommend that the officer place his hand on the offender's shoulder. Such touch will meet the technical requirement of physical control.

While the foregoing represents the technical requirements, courts frequently interpret them liberally according to the circumstances of the particular case and the good faith action of the officers involved.

The right to make an arrest generally depends upon whether the offense is a felony or misdemeanor and the amount of evidence and information that a police officer has regarding its commission.

Arrests may be made either with or without a warrant, depending upon the particular situation. For the purposes of analyzing technical aspects, there are three distinct categories of arrests: (1) arrest for a misdemeanor without a warrant; (2) arrest for a felony without a warrant; and (3) arrest with a warrant.

Excluding traffic offenses, police make well over five million arrests each year. In most major cities misdemeanor arrests will account for 75 to 90 percent of this total.[2] Nationally almost 45 percent of all arrests are for crimes against public order, such as drunkenness, liquor law infractions, and vagrancy. Nationally, arrests for major crimes are approximately 18 to 25 percent of the total.[3] Approximately 90 percent of all arrests are made without warrants.[4]

Arrests Without a Warrant for Misdemeanor Offenses

Under common law, a police officer or a citizen was permitted to arrest without a warrant for a misdemeanor committed in his presence if that misdemeanor constituted a breach of the peace. A breach of the peace meant that the offense was committed with violence or might have caused an immediate disruption or disturbance of public order. Today, either through legislation or judicial interpretation, most states have extended the power of a police officer to permit him to arrest without a warrant for any offense committed in his presence. In approximately twenty states, the citizen's power to arrest has likewise been extended. In other states, the authority of the citizen in misdemeanor cases has remained as it was at common law (i.e., permitting arrests for breach of the peace only); been slightly expanded to include other misdemeanors; or has been totally eliminated.[5]

Most misdemeanor arrests occur when a police officer observes an individual commit an act which constitutes the offense, clearly complying with the "in presence" requirement. However, presence may also include circumstances perceived by the officer through his other senses—hearing, smell, taste, or touch. An example of such extension is found in a Kentucky case:[6]

> . . . the appelant was beating his mistress . . . in an upstairs room occupied by them, in the City of Louisville. Her cries attracted the attention of . . . two policemen . . . and they at once hastened to the house. They located the room where the offense was being committed by the noise, but just before they entered it the appelant stopped beating her, the cries ceased, and they knew of it, therefore, only by hearing and not by sight. The accused . . . [claimed] he had done nothing in their presence and therefore they could not arrest him without a warrant. . . . Unquestionably they had a right to make the arrest. While the offense of beating the woman was not committed in their sight; yet, it was within their hearing, and when they were so near that they could not be mistaken as to the offender. This was within their presence, as contemplated by the law.

A similar case in Michigan upheld an arrest made by officers without a warrant after they heard noises constituting a breach of the peace emitting from a private home. However, in this case the offense continued after the officers' entry into the house.

The "in presence" requirement has been held valid in cases where an officer identified a substance as a prohibited drug by its unique taste, noticed the presence of an illegal alcoholic beverage by its odor, smelled marijuana smoke, and similar circumstances. If the officer physically perceives the event, it normally will be construed to have occurred in his presence.

Although it might appear that arrest without a warrant for a misdemeanor committed in the officer's presence is a relatively simple doctrine, it creates numerous practical problems for police officers in their day-to-day activities. For instance, when the police are called to a private house in response to a marital dispute or a minor assault and battery, in most cases the hostilities have terminated before they arrive. In investigating an automobile accident the police officer relies upon physical evidence at the scene and the statements of participants and witnesses; the offense causing the accident did not occur in his presence. When the owner of a business establishment observes a shoplifter and calls the police, an offense has not occurred in the officer's presence. When a person reports to an officer that his neighbor has been window-peeking, playing the radio too loud, or beating his dog, the officer cannot arrest since these offenses were not committed in his presence.

It is clear that the philosophy of the common law and the general policy of the various state legislatures limit the unilateral arrest power of police on minor offenses. The "in presence" requirement assures a high degree of certainty that the offense did occur before an arrest is made.

When a misdemeanor offense is committed outside the presence of the officer, alternative means are available to bring the offender into court. Witnesses may file a formal complaint before a magistrate and a warrant may be issued for the violator's arrest; under certain circumstances the officer may issue the violator a summons which requires his appearance in court.

In addition to the "in presence" requirement, most states require that the officer take appropriate action to consummate the arrest either immediately or after pursuit. If the officer delays his arrest for an unreasonable length of time, he will be required to obtain a warrant in order to arrest the violator.

Arrest Without a Warrant for Felony Offenses

Common law recognized the authority of a police officer to arrest for a felony without a warrant (1) when it was committed in his presence; (2) upon the oral accusation of another; (3) upon reasonable and probable cause to believe that a felony had been committed and that the person arrested committed it; and (4) for a felony actually committed by the arrested person not in the officer's presence.[7]

There was only one basic distinction in common law between a police officer's authority and that possessed by a citizen. The police officer making an arrest on probable cause to believe a felony had been committed was protected from liability if, in fact, one had not been committed. The private person's only protection was that the felony had in fact been committed and he was in possession of reasonable grounds to believe the arrestee committed it.[8]

Most state legislatures have codified the circumstances under which a police officer may make an arrest without a warrant for a felony. By way of illustration, the Michigan legislature has enacted the following statute:

> Any peace officer may, without a warrant, arrest a person: (A) For the commission of any felony . . . committed in his presence; (B) When such a person has committed a felony although not in the presence of the officer; (C) When a felony has been committed and he has reasonable cause to believe that such person has committed it; (D) When he has reasonable cause to believe that a felony has been committed and reasonable cause to believe such person committed it; (E) When he has received positive information by written, telegraphic, teletypic, telephonic, radio or other authoritative source that another officer holds a warrant for such arrest; (F) When he has received such positive information broadcast from any recognized police or other governmental radio station, or teletype, as may afford him reasonable cause to believe that a felony has been committed and reasonable cause to believe that such person committed it.[9]

Of primary concern in the foregoing statute and in the similar authority of most other states is the provision that an officer may arrest when he possesses reasonable or probable cause to believe both that a felony has been committed and that the arrestee committed it. For practical purposes the other conditions are encompassed within this one provision and merely support it.

In evaluating the validity of a felony arrest without a warrant, the courts have concentrated on whether or not "probable cause" for such arrest existed. Because of the many complexities, the courts have been unable to devise precise, all-encompassing detailed criteria for what constitutes reasonable cause (not that such precision is desirable), but have approached the problem on an *ad hoc* case-by-case basis, utilizing general guidelines. As one court phrased it:

> No exact formula exists for determining reasonable cause to believe the person to be arrested has committed a felony, so as to justify

an arrest without a warrant, and each case must be decided on the facts and circumstances presented to the arresting officers at the time they were required to act.[10]

The United States Supreme Court in adjudicating this question made the following statements:

> In dealing with probable cause, however, as the very name implies, we deal with probabilities. These are not technical; they are factual and practical considerations of every day life on which reasonable and prudent men, not legal technicians, act. . . .
>
> "The substance of all definitions" of probable cause "is a reasonable ground for the belief of guilt" . . . And this "means less than evidence which would justify condemnation" or conviction . . . it has come to mean more than bare suspicion: Probable cause exists where "the facts and circumstances within their [the officer's] knowledge and of which they had reasonable trustworthy information [are] sufficient in themselves to warrant a man of reasonable caution in the belief that" an offense has been or is being committed. . . .
>
> The rule of probable cause is a practical, non-technical conception affording the best compromise that we have found for accommodating these often opposing interests. Requiring more would unduly hamper law enforcement. To allow less would be to leave law-abiding citizens at the mercy of the officer's whim or caprice.[11]

When the constitutional validity of a felony arrest is challenged, it is the function of a court to determine whether the facts available to the officer at the moment of arrest would "warrant a man of reasonable caution in the belief that an offense has been committed."[12]

Clearly, under these guidelines mere suspicion will not justify an arrest. However, these guidelines do not require the officer to have observed the crime, nor do they mean that the officer must have actual personal knowledge. It is not necessary that the officer be able to prove the individual guilty beyond a reasonable doubt. The probable cause required to make an arrest is substantially less than the level of proof required to convict in court. What is evident is that the courts will consider in each case the information available to the officer at the time of the arrest and the general circumstances and conditions surrounding the case. It will then evaluate the adequacy of the information and circumstances by determining what probable conclusions a reasonable and prudent man would reach given the same facts.

Arrest with a Warrant

In cases of arrest without a warrant, the police officer reviews the facts and circumstances and makes a unilateral decision that there are sufficient grounds and legal authority to make the arrest. In cases involving arrests with a warrant, the police officer first submits his evidence to a judge, who, in theory, reviews it and determines if it is sufficient to justify an arrest. If he so determines, he issues a warrant commanding the arrest.

Of primary concern in this process is the Fourth Amendment to the Constitution, which provides:

> The right of the people to be secure in their persons, houses, papers and effects, against unreasonable searches and seizures, shall not be violated, and no Warrants shall issue, but upon probable cause, supported by Oath or affirmation, and particularly describing the place to be searched, and the persons or things to be seized.

Normally, the state constitution will contain a similar provision. The Fourth Amendment and similar state provisions, then, not only regulate unreasonable searches by police officers but also have a direct application to arrests—seizures of persons.

Some authorities take the position that the Fourth Amendment, by inference, requires that all arrests be made with a warrant. This inference is overcome by the common law doctrine of emergency and necessity, permitting arrests without warrants in order to prevent the escape of the felon, or to restore order in cases of breach of peace, and and alterations thereof by legislative enactments expanding arrest powers.

There can be little doubt that the arrest which has been authorized by a warrant after a thorough judicial review is most desirable. To obtain the warrant the police will have presented sufficient evidence to the magistrate to establish probable cause. This process should assure a more objective evaluation than may occur in a hasty determination by the police officer in the field. This judicial blessing places the officer on much firmer legal ground for his action.

Despite the constitutional inference and the many advantages of prior judicial review, only approximately 10 percent of all arrests are made as a result of warrants.[13] Perhaps this is the result of statutory expansion of the common law arrest power coupled with the practical time factors involved. Under most state arrest laws if an officer has sufficient grounds to get a warrant, he may make an arrest without a warrant that is just as legal and much more expedient (with the one exception of a misdemeanor not committed in his presence).

Although the procedure may vary somewhat from state to state, the first step in obtaining the arrest warrant is the preparation of a formal accusation generally known as a complaint. The complaint is a written document which sets forth in legal form the general facts and circumstances of the commission of the crime. The complaint is signed under oath by a police officer, victim, or witness who has knowledge of the facts alleged therein.

The complaint is filed before a magistrate. The magistrate may place the complainant (and possibly other witnesses) under oath and require them to testify concerning the facts alleged in the complaint. The magistrate is responsible then, based upon the complaint and his examination of witnesses, to determine if probable cause exists to arrest the accused and bring him before the court to answer the charge.

Concerning the magistrate's duty in such matters the United States Supreme Court stated:

> The purpose of the complaint . . . is to enable the appropriate magistrate . . . to determine whether the "probable cause" required to support the warrant exists. . . . [The magistrate] must judge for himself the persuasiveness of the facts relied on by a complaining officer to show probable cause. He should not accept without question the complainant's mere conclusions that the person whose arrest is sought has committed a crime.[14]

Mr. Justice Douglas in another case observed:

> I think in these Fourth Amendment cases the duty of the magistrate is nondelegable. It is not sufficient that the police think there is cause for the invasion of the privacy of a home. The judicial officer must also be convinced. . . . The magistrate should know the evidence on which the police propose to act. Unless that is the requirement, unless the magistrate make his independent judgment on all known facts, then he tends to become merely the tool of police interests. Though the police are honest and their aims worthy, history shows they are not appropriate guardians of the privacy which the Fourth Amendment protects.[15]

If the magistrate concludes that probable cause exists he may issue the warrant. The warrant is directed to a police officer for service. The officer consummates the arrest based upon the authority of the warrant. The officer, acting under a warrant, is only executing an order of the court, and so long as he acts in good faith, he is virtually immune from liability.

The following decision of a California court illustrates the protection afforded a police officer by a warrant:

> Where a warrant valid in form and issued by a court of competent jurisdiction is placed in the hands of an officer for execution, it is his duty without delay to carry out its commands. The law is well settled that for proper execution of such process the officer incurs no

liability, however disastrous may be the effects of its execution upon the person against whom it is issued.[16]

Although the warrant may vary in form from one jurisdiction to another, it has a number of common characteristics and requirements:

1. It is a document in writing issued in the name of the geographic jurisdiction. (At common law and in some states today, an arrest may be made on the oral order of a magistrate when the offender has committed or attempted to commit an offense in the presence of the magistrate.)
2. It is normally addressed or directed to a general class of police officers. Under common law a magistrate could direct a warrant to any person. However, most states have abolished this either by statute or common practice.
3. The person or persons to be arrested must be specified with a high degree of certainty. So called "John Doe" warrants, which provide neither name nor adequate identifying characteristics, are void. This doctrine is well stated in the following excerpts from an early Massachusetts case:
   ". . . the warrant . . . was insufficient, illegal and void. It did not contain the name of the defendant, nor any description or designation by which he could be known and identified as the person against whom it was issued. It was in effect a general warrant, upon which any other individual might as well have been arrested. . . . Such a warrant was contrary to the elementary principles, and in direct violation of the constitutional right of the citizen. . . . This rule or principle does not prevent the issue and service of a warrant against a party whose name is unknown. In such case the best description possible . . . is to be given in the warrant; but it must be sufficient to indicate clearly on whom it is to be served, by stating his occupation, his personal appearance and peculiarities, the place of his residence, or other circumstances by which he can be identified."[17]
4. It must specify the offense with which the accused is charged.
5. It commands that the accused be arrested and brought before the magistrate.
6. It indicates the date, the place of issuance, the court of issuance, and is signed by the magistrate. It may also be impressed with the court seal.

Incidental Powers

In order to provide law enforcement officers adequate means to implement effectively a decision to arrest, most state legislatures have specified a number of incidental powers. These include the use of necessary reasonable force in overcoming physical resistance, pursuit of one in flight, the use of deadly force to apprehend a fleeing felony, and breaking and entering a home or other building. The officer is under no duty to retreat and has been endowed with the means of overcoming attempts to thwart the arrest.

Conclusion

Law enforcement officers in most states possess the arrest powers previously discussed. However, the infinite variety of constitutional provisions, statutory enactments, and judicial decisions in the respective states make it extremely difficult to universalize on each point. Therefore, in considering the law of arrest (and for that matter, other areas of legal authority and power) the student should recognize that the generalizations may represent only the preponderance of practices among the states. When a specific jurisdiction is examined, its legislature or its courts may have expanded or contracted the officer's authority.

The authority to arrest endows the police officer with the power to significantly restrict individual liberty. If properly utilized, it is a power which may result in effective law enforcement. Improperly utilized, it may result in irreparable damage.

Discussion Questions

1. Should the citizen and the police officer possess the same powers of arrest?
2. What is "probable cause"?
3. Assume a state legislature passes the following statute: "Any peace officer may, without a warrant, arrest a person when he has probable cause to believe a misdemeanor has been committed and probable cause to believe such person committed it." What are the ramifications of such a statute?
4. What are the advantages of requiring the police officer to have an arrest warrant, both from the standpoint of the police and the citizen?

Chapter Five

The Discretionary Use and Abuse of the Arrest Power

Traditionally, the police officer has been regarded as an individual assigned to perform nothing more than ministerial duties. In theory, the legislature determines what constitutes crime, endows the policeman with enforcement powers, and assigns him to execute all the laws, against all the people, all the time—a policy of full enforcement. In defining duties of the law enforcement officer, legislation almost universally dictates or implies a full enforcement policy. With only very rare exceptions, courts have refused to recognize any authority of the police to vary even slightly from the legislative policy.

Under this theoretical approach the policeman has no decision-making authority—no discretion. He simply determines if he has reasonable grounds to believe a criminal statute has been violated, and if he has the legal authority to take action. On determining that these prerequisites are met, his duty is to initiate appropriate action against the violator.

In practice, however, a totally opposite effect is achieved. For practical purposes, each individual police officer is not ministerial, but administrative, making numerous decisions daily and utilizing the utmost discretion. Commenting on this phenomenon, the President's crime commission indicated:

> At the very beginning of the process—or, more properly, before the process begins at all—something happens that is scarcely discussed in law books and is seldom recognized by the public: law

> enforcement policy is made by the policeman. For policemen cannot and do not arrest all offenders they encounter. It is doubtful that they arrest most of them. A criminal code, in practice, is not a set of specific instructions to policemen but a more or less rough map of the territory in which policemen work. How an individual policeman moves around that territory depends largely upon his personal discretion.[1]

Most legislatures have established the outer boundaries of the police officer's authority to exercise his arrest power. Care has been taken to assure that the authority is sufficiently limited so as not to infringe upon individual freedom unduly. The major thrust of judicial decisions has been directed toward controlling the police officer in making arrests that exceed his lawful authority. Numerous remedies have been provided against the officer who abuses this authority. An accused who has been subjected to an unlawful arrest may bring a civil action for damages or possibly a criminal action for the violation of civil rights. Evidence which has been obtained as a result of an unlawful arrest will in most cases be excluded from use in the trial of the criminal case. More progressive police departments have established procedures for citizen complaints and internal discipline.

Similar control and scrutiny have not been exercised in cases where officers have chosen not to utilize their arrest powers. An individual police officer's decision not to arrest in a specific case is not normally made a subject of public concern or knowledge. Since frequently the crime involves only the officer observing the violator, or an offense in which the victim willingly participated, no objection is raised concerning the officer's decision of inaction. In most such cases, no written report is submitted. These incidents are generally unknown even to the officer's supervisor and if called to his attention he would probably agree with the practice.

An in-depth study of enforcement practices in three states disclosed a number of reasons for policemen choosing a course of nonenforcement. Some of the reasons were:

- The statute was too vague or ambiguous and insufficient legal guidelines were provided. An example of this is pornography and obscenity legislation.
- The statute as formulated by the legislature was overly broad and never intended to be fully enforced. An example of this is the application of gambling statutes to strictly social gambling in an individual's private home, or a church-sponsored bingo game.
- The statute was concerned with reflecting general standards of morality and community ideals, as opposed to having true punitive application. An example of this adultery and fornication statutes.

- The statute is obsolete. An example is a Sunday closing law which has been on the statute books for the last one hundred years, but has not been locally enforced in twenty years.
- The likelihood of prosecution or conviction was extremely weak; or even if a conviction was obtained, the punishment provided by the statute or local custom was either too strict or too lenient. An example of this is drunken driving cases in which traditionally it is extremely difficult to obtain conviction because of the sympathy of jury members. In some states, if a conviction for drunken driving is obtained, a mandatory jail sentence and lengthy suspension of driving privileges results.
- The offense is too trivial, common, and time consuming to enforce fully. Examples are traffic violations, drunkenness, minor juvenile infractions, curfew violations, etc.
- The prohibited conduct is accepted as a part of the regular custom, practice, and prevailing standards of an identifiable subculture. This was noted in areas of cities occupied by racial minority groups. Such acts as felonious assaults on spouses or acquaintances and carrying concealed weapons were frequently subjects of police inaction.
- The victim does not desire to prosecute. In such cases as shoplifting or bad checks, the victim is only interested in recovering his property or receiving restitution for his loss.
- The victim is the offender's wife or a member of his family. One of the most time-consuming tasks of the police department is responding to family disputes. If there is no significant danger to the victim's safety, police generally attempt to avoid arrests.
- The victim himself was involved in improper or criminal conduct. Arrests are frequently avoided in a situation such as that when an individual attempting to obtain the service of a prostitute loses his money through some fraud without obtaining the anticipated service.
- The arrest would tend to create a situation which could result in loss of public respect or public support for the police. In a community where the public tolerates and participates in certain types of illegal activity, such as gambling, a full enforcement policy would tend to create public pressures against the police department.
- The failure to arrest the individual would be helpful to the police department or the individual officer. An example of this is when a police officer overlooks an infraction because the violator is an informant who is providing the police with information concerning a variety of criminal conduct within the community.[2]

The study also found that, on occasion, police officers make arrests for minor offenses which, as a matter of departmental practice, were normally unenforced. Some of the reasons found for this action include:

- Attempting to maintain or coerce respect for the police or the police department. When an individual was discourteous or belligerent, he was frequently arrested. When these circumstances were absent, this step would not have occurred.
- Attempting to give an appearance of full enforcement. Where an individual or a group openly flaunts illegal activity that the police would ignore under most circumstances, arrests are frequently made.
- Punishing an individual who has been involved, or is suspected of being involved, in other types of criminal activity. Officers, faced with a situation in which they cannot obtain sufficient evidence to establish grounds for arrest for the primary violation, arrest the offender on a secondary, minor offense which is normally not enforced.
- Assisting in the investigation of another criminal violation. An arrest provides the officers with custody of the suspect, as well as some collateral powers to search and question. (These powers will be examined in subsequent chapters.) Through the use of this technique investigative advantages are gained.[3]

In addition, the study disclosed that police use the arrest power for purposes other than bringing an offender before a court to stand trial. Intoxicated persons were arrested for their own safety, lodged until they became sober, and released without charge. Mass arrests of known and suspected prostitutes were made. These individuals were detained overnight and subjected to laboratory tests for venereal disease. Those found to be infected were treated. Subsequently they were released without charge or other legal disposition. The arrest, detention, and release practice was also applied to transvestites. While each of these practices is illegal or highly questionable, the rationale given by police was that effective deterrent, rehabilitation, or punitive results were obtained by the practices.[4]

After thorough consideration, very few would advocate a full enforcement policy, or the total elimination of discretion from the police officer's decision. An intolerable situation would exist if the police enforced *all* the laws *all* the time regardless of the surrounding circumstances. In addition to requiring a vast expansion of police resources and an inordinate expenditure of funds, removing discretion from the police officer would result in his operating like a computer, displaying the coldness of a robot. Law enforcement would become a mechanical, dehumanized process, with no concern for the frailties and problems of human beings and the numerous complex social situations in which they may find themselves.

However, improper use of this discretion by members of the police department, even in such minor matters as traffic violations, can create major injustices.

For instance a pilot study, conducted by a sociologist at the University of California at Los Angeles, utilized five white, five Black, and five Mexican-American subjects with no traffic violations within the previous year. After receiving pledges that each would drive as carefully as possible and obey all traffic rules and regulations, Black Panther Party stickers were affixed to the bumpers of their automobiles. Within a period of seventeen days, all fifteen subjects had been ticketed for traffic violations, totalling thirty-three summons, amounting to five hundred dollars in fines.[5]

Even inconsistent, but not improper, use of discretion by police officers can create very reasonable perceptions of bias, prejudice, and favor. A hypothetical, but realistic, set of facts can perhaps better illustrate this point:

- Officer A observes Juvenile X commit a misdemeanor offense. He takes the juvenile into custody and files a petition in juvenile court against him.
- Officer B observes Juvenile Y commit the same misdemeanor under the same general conditions. He takes the juvenile into custody, calls his parents to the police station, and after a long discussion and lecture session, releases the juvenile to his parents without filing a petition.
- Officer C observes Juvenile Z commit the same misdemeanor under the same general conditions. The officer's first inclination is to ignore the offense as he has done many times in the past, but on second thought he stops his car and has a brief talk with the juvenile, warning him not to commit the offense again. He releases the juvenile without even making a notation of the incident.

The hypothetical case may be further complicated by interjecting additional fairly realistic facts:

- Juvenile X has had no previous police record. He has an excellent academic record. He is active socially and is a member of his high school athletic team.
- Juvenile Y has had two previous minor contacts with the police and has been processed by the juvenile court on one occasion. He has an adequate academic record and is active socially.
- Juxenile Z has a lengthy record of police contacts. He has previously been processed through juvenile court on two incidents

of a felonious nature. He is a high school dropout and a member of a local group known for its disruptive influence in the neighborhood.

- The parents of X, Y, and Z all live in the same apartment building or are neighbors. They discuss among themselves the various dispositions made by the police of their children for the same act.

Even though officers A, B, and C were acting with the utmost of good faith in the exercise of their individual discretion, it is difficult, if not impossible, to justify to the parents and other interested parties the different application of personal and subjective criteria to the same offense. If X happens to be a member of a racial minority group, a particular religious sect, or his father is a member of a less dominant political party, additional difficulties are interjected.

Police administrators have generally taken the position that their police departments and officers follow a full enforcement policy and do not exercise discretion. The reasons for such a stance may include:

- A desire for maintaining a public image of totally objective agencies, functioning without fear or favor. This enables them to be in a better position to avoid charges of partiality or favoritism.
- A recognition that the existence of discretion provides greater opportunities for corruption. By failing to recognize and develop policy based upon discretion, it is hoped the opportunities for corruption will not become publicly known.
- A fear that selective enforcement may give rise to legal actions challenging the articulated enforcement policies.
- Many of the practices involved contain at least degrees of illegality and to admit this might require a reexamination and termination of "effective" police techniques.[6]

The Police Task Force of the President's Crime Commission found that the failure of police executives to accept a policy-formulating role concerning the exercise of discretion by members of their departments constituted a significant problem. Its report indicated:

> The results of efforts on the part of individual police officers, under current practice, to improvise their response to many of the situations they confront are often surprisingly good, considering the absence of systematic planning: disputes are resolved; persons are disarmed; people not in control of their capacities are protected; and many are spared what, under the circumstances would appear to be the undue harshness of the criminal process. But there are numerous situations in which mere volume and the lack of guidance result in an officer disposing of incidents less satisfactorily because of the ease with

> which the matter can be disposed of, the officer's personal attitudes toward the victim or the complainant, or his guess as to what form of disposition will most please his immediate supervisor. Similarly, command officers and entire departments will often respond to situations in a manner primarily dictated by pressures exerted by the community, rather than by careful assessment of the competing values involved.
>
> Proper and consistent exercise of discretion in a large organization, like a police department, will not result from the individual judgment of individual police officers in individual cases. Whatever the need for the exercise of judgment by an individual officer may be, certainly the development of overall law enforcement policies must be made at the departmental level and communicated to individual officers. This is necessary if the issues are to be adequately defined and adequately researched and if discretion is to be exercised consistently throughout the department.[7]

Only rarely have police officers been provided with meaningful policies, instructions, or training in the utilization of their discretion. The legislatures have generally phrased their grants or limitations of power in broad terms; the police administrators have taken a course of permitting officers to improvise on a case-by-case basis, and the courts' primary concern has been officers who exceed their arrest power.

For practical purposes, then, the enforcement or nonenforcement of the criminal law and the determination of the means and methods utilized to enforce it (within the outer boundaries set by the legislature and court decisions) are matters for the discretion of police officers in the disposition of individual cases.

This is particularly critical since the police are the initiating agency in an overwhelming majority of criminal cases. Although cases may be originated by a private citizen signing a complaint before a magistrate or prosecuting attorney, or upon indictment after a grand jury investigation, the police remain the primary invokers of the criminal law. The police act; the remainder of the system—prosecutor, defense attorney, trial court, appellate court, etc.—react. The policeman on the street has possession of the ignition switch which starts the machinery of criminal justice into operation, and the machinery is activated at his individual discretion. The obvious consequences may often be unequal justice or blatant injustice.

Discussion Questions

1. While on duty and en route to a local restaurant to take a lunch break, Officer A observes a traffic violation. What alternative courses of action are available to him?

2. Considering the amount of discretion exercised by a police officer, what effect may his personal biases have upon the administration of criminal justice?
3. In the past, the Hypothetical City Police Department has had no standard policy or procedures concerning the issuance of traffic tickets. Its two hundred policemen have utilized their individual discretion on the matter. Is a departmental policy desirable?
4. The Chief of Police of Hypothetical City, in addition to providing regular police services, is faced with major problems of residential burglary, traffic accidents, and street robbery. He does not have sufficient manpower to accomplish all these tasks, and a recent request for more manpower was denied by the city council. What criteria should he utilize in assigning manpower and determining priorities between tasks? Is this a form of discretion?

Chapter Six

Detention Short of Arrest: Field Interrogation and "Stop and Frisk"

Many police agencies utilize a technique known as field interrogation as one means of detecting and/or investigating crime. Field interrogation is a practice of stopping an individual or a group on the street when circumstances or conditions are such that the police officer is generally suspicious of the conduct or activity.

Normally, when a police officer has stopped the individual, he will ask him to provide some means of identification and request that he explain and justify the suspicious circumstances or activity. In most cases the individual complies with the officer's request.

If the individual does not furnish sufficient identification, inadequately explains the questionable circumstances, or refuses to respond to the officer's requests, he receives further attention. In all probability, the officer will detain him longer for additional "on-the-street" inquiry, take him to police headquarters for further investigation, or place him under arrest for the violation of some general ordinance, such as loitering, vagrancy, curfew, etc.

Although this technique (and many variations thereof) has historically been recognized by police as a prime method of aggressive preventive patrol, the practice has virtually been ignored by most legislatures and courts until recent years. Today it has become a sensitive issue, raising the question of the acceptability of police officers interfering with individual liberty without some adequate justification in the form of probable cause.

Extensive field studies conducted in 1956-1957 as a part of the American Bar Foundation's survey of the administration of criminal justice in the United States indicated that the practice of stopping and questioning individuals may serve many different purposes. A few examples follow:

- A police officer suspects that an individual has committed a crime or is about to commit a crime. Although the officer has insufficient grounds to arrest the individual, a stop is made and subsequent events may disclose the criminal activity. Such a stop is for the purpose of apprehension and prosecution.
- A police officer may be aware that a certain area of the community is utilized almost exclusively by prostitutes for plying their trade. He may choose to stop individuals who, he feels, are prospective customers and question them. His concern is more prevention or harassment than arrest and prosecution.
- In areas where there has been a high number of assaults, especially with weapons, the police may undertake a program of indiscriminately stopping individuals on the street, searching them for weapons, confiscating any weapons found, and releasing the individuals. In these cases, the police are concerned more with eliminating the deadly weapons from circulation than with prosecution.
- When a police officer observes an individual immobile in an automobile, he may stop and question him for the purpose of determining if he is intoxicated or is perhaps ill and in need of aid.

Although the American Bar Foundation studies of 1956-1957 may appear dated, a national study conducted by Michigan State University in 1966 indicated that the described practices of the previous decade were still very prevalent.[1]

Some of the described tactics are illegal. Others are of questionable legality. To make the issue even more complex, the tendency is to utilize these strategies in areas where major police-public problems already exist. The President's Crime Commission found: "In many communities, field interrogations are a major source of friction between the police and minority groups. Many minority group leaders strongly contend that field interrogations are predominantly conducted in slum communities, that they are used indiscriminately, and that they are conducted in an abusive and unfriendly manner."[2]

The police consider field interrogation to be an effective means of preventing and solving many types of crimes. Seldom will the police discover a crime in progress. When the officer is dispatched to a crime scene, the offender has normally fled, crowds have formed, and simple apprehension is thwarted. The police believe that prevention is possible if suspicious individuals can be questioned and possibly discouraged from criminal behavior by the encounter.

In 1968 the issue of a police officer detaining ("stopping") and conducting a cursory search ("frisking") was raised before the United States Supreme Court in *Terry* v. *Ohio*.[3] In this case, the facts clearly indicated the good faith and reasonable judgment of the police officer and substantial motivation for his actions. The Court held:

> . . . where a police officer observes unusual conduct which leads him reasonably to conclude in the light of his experience that criminal activity may be afoot and that the person with whom he is dealing may be armed and dangerous; where in the course of investigating this behavior he identifies himself as a policeman and makes reasonable inquiries; and where nothing in the initial stages of the encounter serves to dispel his reasonable fear for his own or others' safety he is entitled for the protection of himself and others in the area to conduct a carefully limited search of the outer clothing of such persons in an attempt to discover weapons which might be used to assault him. Such a search is a reasonable search . . . and any weapons seized may properly be introduced in evidence. . . .

Justice Bryon White in a concurring opinion in the same case, wrote:

> There is nothing in the Constitution which prevents a policeman from addressing questions to anyone on the streets. Absent special circumstance, the person approached may not be detained or frisked but may refuse to cooperate and go on his way. However, given the proper circumstances, . . . it seems to me the person may be briefly detained against his will while pertinent questions are directed to him. Of course, the person stopped is not obliged to answer, answers may not be compelled, and refusal to answer furnishes no basis for an arrest, although it may alert the officer to the need for continued observation. . . .

Being highly concerned about the eroding of Fourth Amendment protections of probable cause, Justice William O. Douglas dissented and indicated such expansion of the police authority was:

> . . . a long step down the totalitarian path. Perhaps such a step is desirable to cope with modern forms of lawlessness. But if it is to be taken, it should be the deliberate choice of the people through constitutional amendment.
>
> Until the Fourth Amendment . . . is rewritten, the person and the effects of the individual are beyond the reach of all government agencies until there are reasonable grounds to believe (probable

> cause) that a criminal venture has been launched or is about to be launched.
>
> There have been powerful hydraulic pressures throughout history that bear heavily on the court to water down constitutional guarantees and give the police the upper hand. That hydraulic pressure has probably never been greater than it is today.
>
> Yet, if the individual is no longer to be sovereign, if the police can pick him up whenever they do not like the cut of his jib, if they can "seize" and "search" him in their discretion, we enter a new regime. The decision to enter it should be made only after a full debate by the people of this country.

In another case, handed down the same day, the Court reversed a conviction, making it relatively clear that the newly endorsed "stop and frisk" policy was not to be regarded as a *carte blanche* discretionary power of the officer.[4] The opinion indicated:

> The police officer is not entitled to seize and search every person whom he sees on the street or of whom he makes inquiries. Before he places a hand on the person of a citizen in search of anything, he must have constitutionally adequate reasonable grounds for doing so. In the case of the self-protective search for weapons, he must be able to point to particular facts from which he reasonably inferred that the individual was armed and dangerous. . . .

These Supreme Court decisions cast some light on the officer's authority, but a close analysis indicates that the decisions are very narrow and leave a considerable number of issues unresolved. The decisions do not give the specific guidelines that police officers, in their daily functioning, require in order to obtain some meaningful balance between crime control techniques and individual rights. Very few police executives have articulated practical policies and procedures. Legislatures, with some minor exceptions, have been relatively silent. For the most part, the decision to stop, question, and/or frisk has been left to the judgment and discretion of the individual officer. The quality of the decision and what consequently occurs on the street is based more on the officer's knowledge, experience, personal attitudes, and his assessment of the particular situation, than on the application of legal or administrative criteria.

The President's Crime Commission made the following observations concerning this lack of guidance:

> The limits of police authority to stop persons briefly for purposes of criminal investigation are unclear in most jurisdictions. In some States, there is a specific statutory authority for officers to stop suspicious persons. . . .

> In most States, however, there is no specific statute which defines this authority. As a result police departments are given little guidance as to when a person may be stopped, whether or how long he may be detained, whether force may be used to detain him, what degree of force may be used, whether a person may be searched, whether he may be compelled to answer certain questions, and under what circumstances he must be advised of his legal rights.
> The Commission believes that there is a definite need to authorize the police to stop suspects and possible witnesses of major crimes, to detain them for brief questioning if they will not cooperate, and to search such suspects for dangerous weapons when such a precaution is necessary.
> In order to balance the need for field interrogations and the harmful effect on police-community relations which may result from their indiscriminate use, State legislatures should define the extent of police authority to stop and question persons, and police departments should adopt detailed policies governing this authority whether or not legislation exists.[5]

No doubt legislators and police administrators recognizing this most pressing need will respond with guidelines. Of prime concern in this area should be the recognition of the principle that simply because a technique is effective does not mean it is desirable. All sides of the questions should be considered, and community attitude and reaction should be a prime factor in the evaluation.

Discussion Questions

1. Frequently, one hears the argument advanced that if a citizen has nothing to hide he doesn't mind being stopped and searched. What is the fallacy in this argument?
2. In what areas of your local community are stop and frisk procedures most likely to be utilized? What results would most likely occur in these areas if an aggressive field interrogation program were utilized?
3. Given only the decision in *Terry* v. *Ohio,* what realistic guidelines and procedures may a police chief formulate for the police department?
4. When there is evidence that a specific police technique is an effective crime prevention tool in a specific community *and* its use has caused significant alienation and hostility toward the police by a large segment of the community, what action should the police administrator take concerning that technique?

Chapter Seven

Searches

The Constitutional Framework Relating to Searches

When an individual is arrested, there invariably is a search of his person. This search frequently extends beyond his person and includes the area where he is arrested and the things under his immediate possession or control. In addition, there are several situations where searches can be made without the individual involved being arrested.

Searches by law enforcement officers are regulated by the Fourth Amendment to the Constitution (which also provides for warrants for arrest). This constitutional provision marks a great change in the concept of legal searches. The common law did not attempt to regulate the conditions under which searches were made. The courts, concerned with adjudicating the defendant's guilt or innocence, did not give significant consideration to how evidence was obtained. If it could be shown that the evidence was competent and relevant to particular issues in the case it was admissable regardless of the means utilized by law enforcement officers in its acquisition.

Even though the Fourth Amendment prohibited "unreasonable searches," the relevancy test for the admissibility of evidence remained in general effect throughout the United States until 1914. In 1914, the United States Supreme Court in *Weeks* v. *United States*[1] exercised its authority to establish rules to supervise the operation of the federal court system and created the "exclusionary rule." The exclusionary rule provided that evidence which was obtained as the result of an unreasonable search was inadmissible in any federal criminal prosecution.

Most state constitutions contain provisions regulating searches by law enforcement officers. Although there may be variations in the language employed, the general thrust of state provisions is identical to the Fourth Amendment. After the Supreme Court established the federal exclusionary rule in the *Weeks* case, a number of states began to examine their own constitutional provisions relating to searches. By 1949, seventeen states had adopted the exclusionary rule. However, thirty states had rejected the rule and continued to permit the admission of evidence under the relevant-trustworthy test.

In 1949, *Wolf* v. *Colorado*[2] raised the question of whether the Fourteenth Amendment due process clause ("nor shall any state deprive any person of life, liberty, or property, without due process of law") required the state courts to exclude evidence obtained by unreasonable searches. The United States Supreme Court held: "in a prosecution in a State court for a State Crime the Fourteenth Amendment does not forbid the admission of evidence obtained by an unreasonable search and seizure."

In its rationale for the *Wolf* decision, the Supreme Court indicated that the Fourth Amendment did not require the exclusion of evidence. The exclusionary rule established for federal cases in *Weeks* was one method of implementing the right against unreasonable searches—and it was the means the Court had chosen for federal jurisdictions. But the Court indicated there were other alternative methods, such as civil actions or criminal prosecutions against the officers conducting the search. The Court, by not imposing the exclusionary rule on the states, permitted them to establish their own alternative procedural safeguards.

Twelve years later, in 1961, the United States Supreme Court in *Mapp* v. *Ohio*[3] overruled *Wolf* and held:

> We hold that all evidence obtained by searches and seizures in violation of the Constitution is, by that same authority, inadmissible in a state court. Since the Fourth Amendment's rights of privacy has been declared enforceable against the States through the Due Process Clause of the Fourteenth, it is enforceable against them by the same sanction of exclusion as is used against the Federal Government . . .

During the period of 1949-1961 the Supreme Court reviewed a number of cases which could have given it strong impressions that state alternatives to the exclusionary rule were ineffective.[4] In justifying its decision in *Mapp* the Court indicated that unless the exclusionary rule was imposed upon the states, the protections and guarantees of the Fourth Amendment remained little more than "an empty promise."

The imposition of the exclusionary rule required the states to meet the federal constitutional standards of "reasonableness." In a subsequent case the Supreme Court held:

> Although the standard of reasonableness is the same under the Fourth and Fourteenth Amendments, the demands of our federal system compel us to distinguish between evidence held inadmissible because of our supervisory powers over federal courts and that held inadmissible because prohibited by the United States Constitution. . . . The States are . . . not precluded from developing workable rules governing . . . searches . . . to meet "the practical demands of effective criminal investigation and law enforcement" . . . provided that those rules do not violate the constitutional prescriptions of unreasonable searches . . . and the concommitant command that evidence so seized is inadmissible.[5]

The Reasonable Search

The Constitution and the Supreme Court's opinions interpreting it do not prohibit all searches—only those which are unreasonable. In determining if a search is reasonable, the facts of the situation, the action of the officers and other parties involved, and all surrounding circumstances seem to be almost as important as the relatively abstract legal theories involved. This was acknowledged in an United States Supreme Court opinion which stated: "what is a reasonable search is not to be determined by any fixed formula. The Constitution does not define what are 'unreasonable' searches and, regretably in our discipline we have no ready litmus-paper test. The recurring question of the reasonableness of searches must find resolution in the fact and circumstances of each case."[6]

Even though there are no specific formulas of reasonableness, there are some general principles which give sound guidance. Searches are generally valid under one of the following conditions:

1. The officer possesses a valid search warrant.
2. The search immediately follows a lawful arrest and includes only the person of the arrestee and that area under his immediate possession and control.
3. The search is made after obtaining voluntary consent of the party involved.
4. An officer has probable cause to believe that a movable vehicle contains property which offends the law ("contraband").

5. The officer, reasonably concluding that a crime may be afoot and that the individual is armed and dangerous while conducting an inquiry, executes a highly limited search for weapons only—"stop and frisk." (See previous chapter.)

6. Where authorized by statute, an officer may conduct specific and limited regulatory searches and inspections.

Search with a Warrant

The Fourth Amendment requires that (1) search warrants may only be issued upon "probable cause" supported by oath or affirmation and (2) the warrant must particularly describe the place to be searched and the things to be seized.

Before a magistrate issues a search warrant, someone must appear before him and under oath sign a "complaint and affidavit for a search warrant." He must testify concerning the facts and information which provide the probable cause to necessitate the search.

If the magistrate decides to issue the warrant it must indicate the specific place to be searched. This requirement is generally met when the description is sufficient to enable the officer executing the warrant to identify the exact location to the distinction and exclusion of all other places.

In a similar manner, the property to be seized must be particularly described. The general requirement is that "as to what is to be taken, nothing is left to the discretion of the officer executing the warrant."[7] More flexible descriptions may be permissible in cases involving contraband, such as narcotics and gambling devices. Where the search relates to private documents or possessions, the description must eliminate discretion.

Legislation and court rules at the state level may establish additional procedures and requirements for obtaining a search warrant. They may provide that the warrant must be executed within a particular time limitation, the methods and force a police officer may use to gain entry, the procedures for detention and search of persons found on the premises, and similar provisions.

The normal procedure for execution of the warrant is for the officer to knock, announce his identity and purpose, and serve a copy of the warrant. Variances in this procedure occur in actual situations; e.g., when the defendant is known to have a gun. Some states have or are contemplating "no knock" legislation where upon sufficient proof of particular circumstances (usually narcotics), the judge may waive certain requirements by so endorsing the warrant.

Officers are limited in the scope and intensity of the search by the circumstances of the case. If the things to be seized are described as "stolen tractor tires with a six-foot diameter," a search of desk drawers, a refrigerator, or book shelves would be unreasonable. On the other hand, searching for a stolen diamond ring or a few ounces of heroin would permit the officers to search much more intensely, both in area and time.

It is quite clear that an officer cannot conduct general exploratory searches under a search warrant. There is a question, however, concerning what action a police officer may take if, during the course of a proper search, he discovers other evidence relating to the search in question or matters relating to another crime. Contradictory cases exist at both the federal and state level on this issue.

In the execution of a search warrant, officers are endowed with the power to protect themselves from attack; to take action against individuals who are interfering with the execution of the warrant; and to use reasonable means to avoid the removal or destruction of property or evidence by others during the search.

If the things described are found they are seized by the officers and an inventory is returned to the court issuing the warrant. Normally, the officer issues a receipt to the person from whom the property was seized, indicating specifically what was taken.

Search Incidental to a Lawful Arrest

The primary justifications given for permitting a search incident to an arrest are (1) protection of the officer and bystanders by removing any weapons, (2) removal of any instrumentalities which might assist an escape, (3) removal of any means of suicide, and (4) preventing the destruction of evidence related to the crime.

It is a well-established legal principle that a police officer, after he has made a lawful arrest, may conduct a search of the person arrested and that area under his immediate possession or control. Historically, the difficulty has been attempting to define specifically what constitutes "immediate possession or control."

In 1947 the Supreme Court accepted as valid the evidence obtained from a search incident to an arrest under a very broad interpretation of the authority. The arrest was made in one room of a four-room apartment. Officers searched the entire four rooms for five hours (for cancelled checks) and ultimately found evidence of another crime (alteration of selective service cards).[8]

After adjudicating numerous cases relating to the question of what constitutes "immediate control," in 1969 the United States Supreme

Court in *Chimel* v. *California*[9] imposed a very strict definition. The opinion stated:

> When an arrest is made, it is reasonable for the arresting officer to search the person arrested in order to remove any weapons that the latter might seek to use in order to resist arrest or effect escape. . . . In addition, it is entirely reasonable for the officer to search for and seize any evidence on the arrestee's person in order to prevent its concealment or destruction. And the area into which an arrestee might reach in order to grab a weapon or evidentiary item must . . . be governed by a like rule. . . . There is ample justification . . . for a search of the arrestee's person and the area "within his immediate control"—construing that phrase to mean the area from within which he might gain possession of a weapon or destructible evidence.
>
> There is no . . . justification . . . for routinely searching rooms other than that in which an arrest occurs—or, for that matter, for searching through all desk drawers or other closed or concealed areas in the room itself.

In order for a search incident to an arrest to be valid, the arrest itself must be lawful. If the officer's arrest is unlawful for any reason, the incidental search will likewise become unlawful.

The arrest must not contain elements of subterfuge. For instance, officers who have ample opportunity to arrest the accused in the public street outside his home but permit him to enter his home and then make the arrest to have an opportunity to conduct an incidental search in the house are performing improperly.

The search must be contemporaneous with the arrest. The arrest must be made first and be immediately followed by the search. In an emergency situation, the search must be made "as soon as practical" and still be within a reasonable time frame. Normally, if the search precedes the arrest it is invalid. However, in an emergency situation, such as when the individual to be arrested is in the process of destroying evidence, the officer is permitted to secure the evidence before formalizing the arrest.

Under normal conditions minor infractions, where the offender usually receives only a summons, such as traffic violations, do not justify a search. However, given circumstances where the officer has cause to believe the defendant is armed, a limited weapons search is permissible.

To be valid the search must be incident to the arrest in purpose, time, place, and scope. Under current rulings the officer may conduct a complete search of the person arrested. He may search things within the individual's actual possession, such as a briefcase, purse, or carton that the arrestee is carrying. He may search the area under the arrestee's immediate control, construing this under *Chimel* to mean "the area into which the arrestee might reach." When the officer goes beyond these limited areas and utilizes only the search authority incidental to arrest, his search is, at best, of doubtful validity.

Consent Searches

Although an individual has a constitutional right not to be subjected to unreasonable searches, if he chooses he may waive that right and consent to the search, even though the police officers have no probable cause either to arrest or obtain a search warrant. The general requirement is that the individual must have voluntarily and intelligently waived the right.

The major difficulty in determining the validity of a consent search is that very few meaningful criteria exist for evaluation. The United States Supreme Court has examined this question only infrequently and indirectly. In *Bumper* v. *North Carolina*[10] the Supreme Court held: "when a prosecutor seeks to rely upon consent to justify the lawfulness of a search, he has the burden of proving that consent was in fact freely and voluntarily given."

The right to be free from an unreasonable search is considered a personal right. Normally, only the individual himself may grant the permission to search. Thus, the United States Supreme Court has held that a landlord cannot give permission to the police to search a tenant's residence,[11] nor could a hotel clerk validly consent to the search of a hotel guest's room. [12] However, the law is not perfectly clear in all cases on the permissibility of third-party consent. Court decisions in some states have permitted the wife to consent to the search of the home when the husband is the suspect. Others have permitted similar third-party consent in the relationships of parent-child, school official-student, bailor-bailee, and joint ownership of property. Other states have rejected these same types of consent.

In asking permission to conduct a search, police seldom advise the suspect of his Fourth Amendment right or inform him that he may refuse. The law at this time is unsettled as to whether this is required. Some jurisdictions have held it unnecessary while others have held it to be a prerequisite. Considering recent Supreme Court decisions and the general concern it has shown over police techniques related to self-incrimination, it is quite possible that informing a suspect of these rights may ultimately be required. For in the absence of some degree of coercion, as one court phrased it: "no sane man who denies his guilt would actually be willing that a policeman search his room for contraband which is certain to be discovered."[13]

From the standpoint of legality, officers conducting a search based solely on consent have chosen the weakest alternative method of obtaining evidence, since the courts will "indulge every reasonable presumption against waiver of fundamental constitutional rights."[14]

Movable Vehicle with Contraband

If a police officer has reasonable cause to believe that a moving or movable vehicle contains contraband, he may conduct a search of the vehicle. The right to search under these circumstances is not dependent on the right to make an arrest.[15]

Contraband for this purpose includes any physical item which offends the law—narcotics, untaxed liquor, gambling equipment, instrumentalities used in the commission of a crime, or fruits of a crime.

This rule has great significance in cases where possession of the contraband is a misdemeanor. In the typical misdemeanor case, the offense must be committed in the officer's presence before he can arrest and conduct an incidental search. However, under the movable vehicle rule, all that is necessary to justify the search is reasonable cause to believe the contraband is present. The authority to search the vehicle under this rule does not automatically confer the power to search or arrest the occupants of the vehicle.

The primary justification for this rule is the impracticalities involved in obtaining a search warrant since the vehicle can be quickly moved out of the locality while a warrant is being sought.

The police seldom use this rule to justify a search either because it is not well known to them or because most searches may be made under other permissable alternatives.

Administrative and Regulatory Searches

Numerous states and subunits thereof have adopted codes establishing minimal standards for housing, health, sanitation, and fire prevention. Most of these directly affect the private home. In addition, certain activities and businesses are required to meet specific standards. The state may license businesses such as liquor establishments, meat-processing plants, barber shops, taxicab companies, and similar enterprises. Frequently, the legislation provides that the home or business may be inspected to determine if the minimal standards of the code are being met.

Inspections of this nature have traditionally been regarded as administrative or regulatory searches, not directed at an individual, but concerned primarily with public health, safety, welfare, and the elimination of public nuisances.

For many years these types of searches were more or less deemed to be an exception to Fourth Amendment search and seizure requirements. However, recent cases have held that such inspections are protected by the Fourth Amendment. While recognizing that "most citizens allow inspections of their property without a warrant," the Supreme Court held that the inspector should first request entry, but if refused he must obtain a search warrant before inspecting a private home.[16] Considering the same problem relating to commercial establishments the Supreme Court held: "administrative entry, without consent upon the portions of commercial premises which are not open to the public may only be compelled . . . within the framework of a warrant procedure."[17]

The acceptable procedure for inspection of the private home is for the inspector to request permission and, upon being denied admittance, to obtain a search warrant. The same restriction applies to a commercial establishment, except a denial is not a prerequisite to obtaining a warrant.

Other types of administrative searches include border searches as individuals enter the country or pass from state to state; searches made in the supervision of parolees from prison; the inspection of dormitory rooms on a college campus in aid of discipline and maintaining an educational atmosphere; driver licenses and vehicle inspection safety checks, etc. Generally, these inspections have been held valid even though conducted without consent and without a warrant, so long as the inspectors have acted within the limited purposes for which the search was authorized.

The Plain-View Doctrine

When a police officer is not a trespasser—when he is in a place where he has a right to be—he is not guilty of an illegal search if he sees something that constitutes contraband or gives him grounds to make an arrest. If the officer is not a trespasser, his eyes alone cannot commit an illegal search. The United States Supreme Court reaffirmed this longstanding doctrine in 1968: "objects falling in the plain view of an officer who has a right to be in the position to have that view are subject to seizure and may be introduced into evidence"[18]

Therefore, if a police officer in the routine process of issuing a traffic ticket observes gambling equipment or untaxed liquor laying on the back seat of the automobile, he may take action. If an officer makes an entry into a home or business for a lawful purpose and observes contraband, it may be seized. However, if an officer crosses a person's yard to peer into his window, such a situation would be outside the scope of the plain-view rule.

Searches by Private Person

The Fourth Amendment restrictions are applicable only to action by governmental officials and not by private citizens. When a private citizen unlawfully seizes evidence without collusion or knowledge of the police, the evidence will not be excluded. The citizen, however, may himself become the defendant in a criminal or civil action as a result of his activity.

Abandoned Property

If a person clearly abandons property, it is no longer protected by the Fourth Amendment. In *Abel v. United States,* where the defendant had thrown several items into a wastebasket and subsequently checked out of his hotel room, entry into the room and seizure of the wastebasket's contents by an F.B.I. agent with the consent of the hotel management was deemed not protected by the Fourth Amendment.[19]

Conclusion

Through the imposition of the exclusionary rule, the Fourth Amendment prohibition of unreasonable search has become a very viable restriction on police practices. While numerous technical questions remain unanswered, it is quite clear that cognizance of high duty is imposed upon the police officer considering undertaking a search. He must do so with extreme care and diligence, exercising due care to preserve individual rights involved. When circumstances make it feasible, the warrant procedure is the most desirable alternative. When the warrant procedure is impractical because of specific factors in the case, the officer acts at his peril if the general guidelines of reasonableness are exceeded. It becomes obvious after overviewing the law of search that the police officer must not only be a skilled, educated technician, but must also possess the ability to apply relatively abstract legal principles to practical factual circumstances, sometimes making these critical judgments in a matter of seconds.

Discussion Questions

1. The exclusionary rule is not required by the Constitution, but has been established as one method of implementing the right to be free from unreasonable searches. What other alternative methods might prove just as effective?
2. Some authorities have indicated the *Mapp* case, in effect, established a federal code of criminal procedures applicable to the states.

If this is true, what are the advantages and disadvantages of such a situation from a state's point of view?

3. In one opinion the United States Supreme Court stated: "what is a reasonable search is not determined by any fixed formula . . . we have no ready litmus-paper test. The recurring question of the reasonableness of searches must find resolution in the facts and circumstances of each case. . . ." Given this condition, how may police officers be trained or educated in the laws of search and seizure?
4. What are the disadvantages of "no knock" laws?
5. Should searches by private persons, not affiliated or in collusion with police, be subjected to the exclusionary rule?

Chapter Eight

Interrogating the Accused

In recent years the standard police practice of questioning the accused subsequent to his arrest has become the subject of significant controversy. The United States Supreme Court, under Chief Justice Earl Warren, established major procedural requirements. Subsequently the Court, under Chief Justice Warren Burger, has made more conservative modifications. The Congress of the United States has attempted to nullify some of the Court's decisions. Local police and prosecutors have been forced to make adjustments in their case preparation techniques. Newspapers and popular magazines focusing on these events have brought the general public's attention to the problem. At the heart of the emotionally laden debate is the question of whether police efficiency should, in some degree, be sacrificed to enhance individual rights.

Numerous authorities take the position that many serious crimes, regardless of how well they might otherwise be investigated, are solvable only with an admission or confession.[1] Others clearly point out that to empower the police to conduct extensive questioning without close supervision will result in the accused's being deprived of his right against self-incrimination.[2]

The issues were well summarized by Supreme Court Justice Felix Frankfurter in the plurality opinion in *Culombe* v. *Connecticut*:[3]

Despite modern advances in the technology of crime detection, offenses frequently occur about which things cannot be made to speak. And where there cannot be found innocent human witnesses to such offenses, nothing remains—if police investigation is not to be balked before it has fairly begun—but to seek out possible guilty witnesses and ask them questions, witnesses, that is, who are suspected of knowing something about the offense precisely because they are suspected of implication in it.

The questions which these suspected witnesses are asked may serve to clear them. They may serve, directly or indirectly, to lead the police to other suspects than the persons questioned. Or they may become the means by which the persons questioned are themselves made to furnish proofs which will eventually send them to prison or death. In any event, whatever the outcome, such questioning is often indispensable to crime detection. . . .

But persons who are suspected of crime will not always be unreluctant to answer questions put by the police. Since under the procedures of Anglo-American criminal justice they cannot be constrained by legal process to give answers which incriminate them, the police have resorted to other means to unbend their reluctance, lest criminal investigation flounder. Kindness, cajolery, entreaty, deception, persistent cross-questioning, even physical brutality have been used to this end. In the United States, "interrogation" has become a police technique, and detention for purposes of interrogation a common, although generally unlawful, practice. Crime detection officials, finding that if their suspects are kept under tight police control during questioning they are less likely to be distracted, less likely to be recalcitrant and, of course, less likely to make off and escape entirely, not infrequently take such suspects into custody for "investigation."

This practice has its manifest evils and dangers. Persons subjected to it are torn from the reliances of their daily existence and held at the mercy of those whose job it is—if such persons have committed crimes, as it is supposed they have—to convict them for it. . . . What actually happens to them behind the closed door of the interrogation room is difficult if not impossible to ascertain. Certainly, if, through excess of zeal or aggressive impatience or flaring up of temper in the face of obstinate silence, a prisoner is abused, he is faced with the task of overcoming by his lone testimony, solemn official denials. The prisoner knows this—knows that no friendly or disinterested witness is present—and the knowledge may itself induce fear. But, in any case, the risk is great that the police will accomplish behind their closed door precisely what the demands of our legal order forbid: make a suspect the unwilling collaborator in establishing his guilt. This they may accomplish, not only with ropes and a rubber hose, not only by relay questioning persistently, insistently subjugating a tired mind, but by subtler devices.[4]

In the police station a prisoner is surrounded by known hostile forces. He is disoriented from the world he knows and in which he finds support. He is subject to coercing impingements. . . . In such an atmosphere, questioning that is long continued—even if it is only repeated at intervals, never protracted to the point of physical exhaustion—inevitably suggests that the questioner has a right to expect an answer. This is so, certainly when the prisoner has never been told he need not answer and when, because his commitment to custody seems to be at the will of his questioners, he has every reason to believe that he will be held and interrogated until he speaks.

However, a confession made by a person in custody is not always the result of an overborne will. The police may be midwife to a declaration naturally born of remorse, or relief, or desperation, or calculation. If that is so, if the "suction process" has not been at the prisoner and drained his capacity for freedom of choice, does not the awful responsibility of the police for maintaining the peaceful order of society justify the means which they have employed? . . .

The critical elements of the problem may be quickly isolated in light of what has already been said. Its first pole is the recognition that "Questioning suspects is indispensable in law enforcement." . . . But if it is once admitted that questioning of a suspect is permissible, whatever reasonable means are needed to make the questioning effective must also be conceded to the police. Often prolongation of the interrogation period will be essential, so that a suspect's story can be checked and, if it proves untrue, he can be confronted with the lie; if true, released without charge. Often the place of questioning will have to be a police interrogation room, both because it is important to assure the proper atmosphere of privacy and non-distraction if questioning is to be made productive, and because, where a suspect is questioned but not taken into custody, he—and in some cases his associates—may take prompt warning and flee the premises. Legal counsel for the suspect will generally prove a thorough obstruction to the investigation. Indeed, even to inform the suspect of his legal right to keep silent will prove an obstruction. Whatever fortifies the suspect or seconds him in his capacity to keep his mouth closed is a potential obstacle to the solution of crime.

At the other pole is a cluster of convictions, each expressive, in a different manifestation, of the basic notion that the terrible engine of the criminal law is not to be used to overreach individuals who stand helpless against it. Among these are the notions that men are not to be imprisoned at the unfettered will of their prosecutors, nor subjected to physical brutality by officials charged with the investigation of crime. Cardinal among them, also, is the conviction, basic to our legal order, that men are not to be exploited for the information necessary to condemn them before the law. . . . This principle, branded into the

> consciousness of our civilization by the memory of the secret inquisitions, sometimes practiced with torture, which were borrowed briefly from the continent during the era of the Star Chamber, was well known to those who established the American government. Its essence is the requirement that the State which proposes to convict and punish an individual produce the evidence against him by the independent labor of its officers, not by the simple, cruel expedient of forcing it from his own lips. . . .

Historically, the primary test for the establishment of validity of a confession admitted into evidence at a criminal trial was whether the confession was voluntary and trustworthy. Voluntary, for these purposes, meant that no physical force was utilized in obtaining the confession. Trustworthy meant that the circumstances under which the confession was obtained were unlikely to induce an innocent man to confess.

Under the voluntary-trustworthy test the length of time the suspect was detained before taking him to court or filing charges did not automatically invalidate a confession obtained during that time. The suspect could be extensively questioned, so long as the circumstances were not such that he became physically exhausted. It was not highly relevant as to whether or not he had an opportunity to consult with an attorney, family, or friends. Officers were free to utilize various techniques, tricks, and devices so long as no physical force was involved and their methods were not designed to induce the confession from an innocent man. This test was applied in both the state and federal courts until 1943.

In 1943 in *McNabb* v. *United States*[5] the United States Supreme Court expanded the voluntary-trustworthy test for federal cases and established an additional test requiring "civilized interrogation standards." In that case federal officers arrested five suspects for the murder of a federal revenue agent who had been in the process of searching for untaxed whiskey. Contrary to a federal statute which provided that after arrest the defendant must be taken without unnecessary delay before a judicial official for a hearing and commitment or bail, the officers detained and questioned the suspects for over two days before obtaining confessions. The Court held:

> Judicial supervision of the administration of criminal justice in the federal courts implies the duty of establishing and maintaining civilized standards of procedure and evidence. . . . Plainly, a conviction resting on evidence secured through such a flagrant disregard of the procedure which Congress has commanded cannot be allowed to stand without making the courts themselves accomplices in willful

> disobedience of law. Congress has not explicitly forbidden the use of evidence so procured. But to permit such evidence to be made the basis of a conviction in the federal courts would stultify the policy which Congress has enacted into law.

In 1957, in *Mallory* v. *United States*[6] the defendant confessed the commission of a rape after being detained by police for a period of seven and one-half hours. The United States Supreme Court in holding the confession inadmissible stated:

> The scheme for initiating a federal prosecution is plainly defined. The police may not arrest upon mere suspicion but only on "probable cause." The next step in the proceeding is to arraign the arrested person before a judicial officer as quickly as possible so that he may be advised of his rights and so that the issue of probable cause may be promptly determined. The arrested person may, of course, be "booked" by the police. But he is not to be taken to police headquarters in order to carry out a process of inquiry that lends itself, even if not so designed, to eliciting damaging statements to support the arrest and ultimately his guilt.
>
> The duty enjoined upon arresting officers to arraign "without unnecessary delay" indicates that the command does not call for mechanical or automatic obedience. Circumstances may justify a brief delay between arrest and arraignment, as for instance, where the story volunteered by the accused is susceptible of quick verification through third parties. But the delay must not be of a nature to give opportunity for extraction of a confession.

The *McNabb-Mallory* rules now require that before a confession may be validly admitted into evidence it must be (1) voluntary, (2) trustworthy, (3) obtained under civilized standards of interrogation, and (4) not obtained during an unnecessary delay between the time of arrest and taking the accused before a magistrate.[7]

The *McNabb-Mallory* rule was applied only to federal cases. Most states have legislation or constitutional provisions similar to the federal rule requiring that the prisoner be taken before a magistrate without unreasonable delay. However, the states, with the exception of Michigan, have not construed this procedural requirement to have direct effect upon the validity and admissibility of the statute. Therefore, the state courts have rejected the *McNabb-Mallory* rule and continue to subscribe to the voluntary-trustworthy test as far as delay between arrest and taking before the magistrate is concerned. Of course, this delay may be considered by the state courts in determining whether the confession is voluntary and trustworthy.

The United States Supreme Court reviewed its first state case involving the admissibility of confession in 1936 in *Brown* v. *Mississippi*.[8] In this case a local sheriff forced two prisoners to lay naked over chairs and beat them with a leather strap with metal buckles to obtain confessions. The Supreme Court found the confession not to be voluntary and utilizing the Fourteenth Amendment "due process" clause reversed the conviction.

In some three dozen cases following *Brown*, the United States Supreme Court scrutinized state court admission of confessions and developed a standard under the due process clause which required an examination of "the totality of the circumstances" involved in the case. The process is described by Justice Brennan in the majority opinion in *Malloy* v. *Hogan* in 1964:

> *Brown v. Mississippi* . . . was the first case in which the Court held that the Due Process Clause prohibited the States from using the accused's coerced confessions against him. The Court in *Brown* felt impelled . . . to say that its conclusion did not involve the privilege against self-incrimination. . . . But this distinction was soon abandoned, and today the admissibility of a confession in a state criminal prosecution is tested by the same standard applied in federal prosecutions . . . [namely] "in criminal trials, in the courts of the United States, wherever a question arises whether a confession is incompetent because not voluntary, the issue is controlled by that portion of the Fifth Amendment to the Constitution of the United States commanding that no person shall be compelled in any criminal case to be a witness against himself." Under this test, the constitutional inquiry is not whether the conduct of state officers in obtaining the confession was shocking, but whether the confession was "free and voluntary"; that is it must not be extracted by any sort of threats or violence, nor obtained by any direct or implied promises, however slight, nor by the exertion of any improper influence. . . . In other words the person must not have been compelled to incriminate himself. We have held inadmissible even a confession secured by so mild a whip as the refusal, under certain circumstances, to allow a suspect to call his wife until he confessed. . . . The shift reflects recognition that the American system of criminal prosecution is accusatorial, not inquisitorial, and the Fifth Amendment privilege is its essential mainstay. . . .
>
> The Fourteenth Amendment secures against state invasion the same privileges that the Fifth Amendment guarantees against federal infringement—the right of a person to remain silent unless he chooses to speak in the unfettered exercise of his own will, and to suffer no penalty . . . for such silence. . . .[9]

In 1964, the Supreme Court in *Escobedo* v. *Illinois*[10] held inadmissible a confession obtained after the police had failed to advise a prisoner of his "absolute constitutional right to remain silent" and had refused to honor the defendant's request to consult with his attorney. In 1966 in *Miranda* v. *Arizona*[11] the Court expanded the doctrine further and in effect established a series of procedural prerequisites that must be met before any interrogation of the arrestee could occur:

> . . . if a person in custody is to be subjected to interrogation he must first be informed in clear and unequivocal terms that he has the right to remain silent. . . .
> The warning of the right to remain silent must be accompanied by the explanation that anything said can and will be used against the individual in court. . . . an individual held for interrogation must be clearly informed that he has the right to consult with a lawyer and to have the lawyer with him during interrogation. . . . it is necessary to warn him not only that he has the right to consult with an attorney, but also that if he is indigent a lawyer will be appointed to represent him. . . . .
> Once warning has been given, the subsequent procedure is clear. If the individual indicates in any manner, at any time prior to or during questioning, that he wishes to remain silent, the interrogation must cease.

It should be noted that both *Escobedo* and *Miranda* were 5-4 decisions. When decisions are made on such narrow margins, divisiveness and polarity on the basic issues are given added impetus throughout society. Following are excerpts from dissenting opinions in these cases.

Justice White dissenting in *Miranda* v. *Arizona:*

> . . . Judged by any of the standards for empirical investigation utilized in the social sciences the factual basis for the Court's premises is patently inadequate. . . ."

Justice Harlan dissenting in *Miranda* v. *Arizona:*

> . . . the practical effect of the decision made today must inevitably be to handicap seriously sound efforts at reform, not least by removing options necessary to a just compromise of competing interest. . . .
> . . . Nothing in the letter or the spirit of the Constitution or in the precedents squares with the heavy handed and one-sided action that is so precipitously taken by the Court in the name of fulfilling its constitutional responsibilities. . . .

Justice White dissenting in *Escobedo* v. *Illinois:*

> . . . The right to counsel now not only entitles the accused to coun-

> sel's advice and aid in preparing for trial but stands as an impenetrable barrier to any interrogation once the accused becomes a suspect. From that very moment apparently his right to counsel attaches a rule wholly unworkable unless police cars are equipped with public defenders and undercover agents and police informants have defense counsel at their side. . . . Under this new approach one might just as well argue that a potential defendant is constitutionally entitled to a lawyer before, not after he commits a crime, since it is then that crucial incriminating evidence is put within the reach of the government by the would be accused. . . .
>
> I do not suggest for a moment that law enforcement will be destroyed by the rule announced today. . . . But it will be crippled and its task made a great deal more difficult . . . for unsound, unstated reasons, which can find no home in any of the provisions of the Constitution.

In June 1968, the United States Congress enacted the *Omnibus Crime Control and Safe Street Act of 1968,* which attempts to alter the admissibility standards of the *McNabb-Mallory* and *Escobedo-Miranda* rulings as applied in federal prosecutions. The Act provides:

> In any criminal prosecution brought by the United States or by the District of Columbia, a confession . . . shall be admissible in evidence if it is voluntarily given. Before such confession is received in evidence, the trial judge shall, out of the presence of the jury, determine any issue as to voluntariness. If the trial judge determines that the confession was voluntarily made it shall be admitted in evidence and the trial judge shall permit the jury to hear relevant evidence on the issue of voluntariness and shall instruct the jury to give such weight to the confession as the jury feels it deserves under all the circumstances. . . . The trial judge in determining the issue of voluntariness shall take into consideration all the circumstances surrounding the giving of the confession, including (1) the time elapsing between arrest and arraignment of the defendant making the confession, if it was made after arrest and before arraignment, (2) whether such defendant knew the nature of the offense with which he was charged or of which he was suspected at the time of making confession, (3) whether or not such defendant was advised or knew that he was not required to make any statement and that such statement could be used against him, (4) whether or not such defendant had been advised prior to questioning of his right to the assistance of counsel; and (5) whether or not such defendant was without the assistance of counsel when questioned and when giving such confession.
>
> The presence or absence of any of the above-mentioned factors to be taken into consideration by the judge need not be conclusive on the issue of voluntariness of the confession. . . . a confession made . . . while such person was under arrest or other detention . . . shall not be inadmissible solely because of delay in bringing such person

> before a commissioner or other officer empowered to commit persons . . . if such confession is found by the trial judge to have been made voluntarily and if the weight to be given the confession is left to the jury and if such confession was made or given by such person within six hours immediately following his arrest or other detention: *Provided,* That the time limitation . . . shall not apply in any case in which the delay in bringing such person before such commissioner or other officer beyond such six-hour period is found by the trial judge to be reasonable considering the means of transportation and the distance to be traveled to the nearest available such commissioner or other officer.

Thus far, the act has not been constitutionally tested but if it were held valid it would invalidate the *McNabb-Mallory* and *Escobedo-Miranda* rulings. It would establish "voluntariness" as the test of admissibility of confessions in federal cases predicated on the court's determination of voluntariness by viewing the totality of the circumstances involved, including delay, lack of attorney, and other considerations.

In February 1971 in *Harris* v. *New York*[12] the United States Supreme Court held in a 5-4 decision that a confession obtained in violation of the *Miranda* principles could be used by the prosecution for a limited purpose. In *Harris* the defendant testified in his own behalf and related a story which was different from that he had given to the police. The prosecutor used the defendant's statement (obtained in violation of *Miranda*) for the sole purpose of cross-examining the defendant and impeaching his testimony. The court found the use of the otherwise tainted confession valid for this limited purpose. While this decision examined in its own context is relatively insignificant, it does have significant implications as precedent for further erosion of the strict exclusionary rule established by *Miranda.*

Summary of the Law Relating to Admissibility of Confessions

1. A confession may be inadmissible because it is obtained under circumstances that do not comply with the voluntary-trustworthy test. Such circumstances would include the use of physical force, promises of leniency, threats, withholding medical treatment from an addict, questioning a person who is ill and extremely weak, and other situations involving inherent coercion.

2. A confession may be inadmissible in federal courts (and Michigan) if obtained during an unreasonable delay after the arrest and prior to taking the accused before a magistrate.

3. A confession may be inadmissible if the defendant requests and is denied counsel during the interrogation stage.

4. A confession may be inadmissible if the officer fails to warn the prisoner that he has a right to remain silent, that anything said can and will be used against him, that he has a right to have counsel present during the interrogation, and that if he is indigent counsel will be provided for him by the state.

5. A confession may be inadmissible if it is obtained as a direct result of an unlawful arrest or an unreasonable search.

The Effects of United States Supreme Court Rulings on Confessions

The *Malloy, McNabb, Escobedo,* and *Miranda* cases clearly illustrate the tremendous influence the United States Supreme Court and other appellate courts can exert on changing the procedural law. Over the past few years the Supreme Court and courts generally have been accused of "coddling criminals" and turning them loose to prey on society. One of the more critical comments was by Justice White in his dissenting opinion in *Miranda:* "In some unknown number of cases the Court's rule will return a killer, a rapist or other criminal to the streets and to the environment which produced him, to repeat his crime whenever it pleases him. As a consequence, there will not be a gain, but a loss, in human dignity."

To justify this position critics of the decisions frequently follow the career of individuals who have obtained reversal in the Courts. For instance, following *Mallory*'s release in 1957, he was arrested in the District of Columbia in 1958 for house-breaking, assault with a dangerous weapon, and simple assault, and ultimately convicted of simple assault and sentenced to sixty days and a hundred-dollar fine. In 1960 he was tried in Philadelphia for rape and burglary, convicted of burglary and aggravated assault, and sentenced to twenty years for burglary and eighteen months to three years for assault, sentences to run consecutively. Three other burglary indictments were outstanding against him at the time. He was released from prison in 1971 and was subsequently killed in a gun battle with a Philadelphia police officer in 1972. The *McNabbs* were convicted on their second trial. *Escobedo,* subsequent to his release in 1964, was arrested and acquitted in 1965 for possession of barbiturates; arrested in March, 1966 and acquitted for carrying a concealed weapon, a gun; arrested in November, 1966 for burglary and disorderly conduct; arrested in September, 1967 for an alleged violation of the federal narcotic law, and was convicted and sentenced to serve twenty years. *Miranda* was convicted on his second trial.

Others argue strongly that the rulings make law enforcement ineffective and result in "handcuffing the police." An example of such position is found in Justice Clark's dissent in *Miranda:* "Such a strict constitutional specific inserted at the nerve center of crime detection may well kill the patient."

The limited number of studies which have been made on the practical impact of the *Escobedo* and *Miranda* decisions, when compared to each other, tend to establish no clear-cut universal effect, and in some cases are contradictory.

In Detroit murder cases the rate of confessions increased in 1965, after the police department established a system of warning suspects of their constitutional rights as required by *Escobedo.*[13]

A study in Pittsburgh indicated that confessions obtained by the police department's detective bureau significantly decreased after *Miranda,* but because of technical problems the researchers were unable to verify the effect this had on conviction rates.[14] Similarly, significant decreases in the number of confessions occurred in New York County, Philadelphia, and Cook County, Illinois.[15]

A study in Washington, D.C. by the Institute of Criminal Law Procedure of the Georgetown University Law Center concluded that no significant changes in confession practices or patterns had occurred subsequent to *Miranda.*[16]

A study by the District Attorney of Los Angeles County concluded that the number of cases necessitating confession for successful prosecution are few. The study also concluded that police officers were following the standards established by *Miranda* and that the percentage of cases where the defendant confessed or made an admission had not decreased. The study did point out that the requirements could be harmful by thwarting a confession at the first meeting between the officer and the suspect, thereby depriving the officer of grounds for arrest—but this was concededly unmeasurable. General compliance with *Miranda* was not found to create significant difficulties.[17]

Research and observation conducted by law students during an eleven-week period the summer following the *Miranda* decision indicated that the warning did not appear substantially to reduce the amount of talking done by suspects. However, observations of New Haven police officers indicated that less than half of the arrestees were advised that anything they said could be used against them; and that the complete *Miranda* warnings were given to less than one-fourth of the prisoners.[18]

Although these studies cannot be totally rationalized, it appears that *Escobedo* and *Miranda* have not had their predicted crippling effect on law enforcement. It would also appear that their provisions may not be as effective in overcoming "the coercive interrogation atmosphere" as some had speculated. Regardless, the temper of the times makes it obvious that the debate over the issues involved will not be rapidly resolved.

Discussion Questions

1. Do more restrictive interrogation procedures result in better case preparation by police? Did police reliance upon confessions prior to court restrictions result in less professionally conducted investigations?
2. Are the many claims that unrestricted interrogation of suspects is prerequisite to some types of crime solution valid?
3. A lawyer's first advice to his arrested client will probably be: "Don't say anything." If this is done in all arrest cases, could the clients suffer? In some cases, may the accused gain advantage by submitting to interrogation?
4. Is it the responsibility of police to obtain convictions? Should one measure of police efficiency be the number of convictions obtained? If so, what inherent dangers are present?

Chapter Nine

Prosecution

Alternative Methods of Prosecution

There are three practical alternative systems of initiating and prosecuting criminal cases. The state, exercising its police power, can establish a system permitting the victim (or in the case of his death, a relative) to initiate proceedings independently. A second method is the establishment of a public prosecutor who possesses the exclusive right and power to commence criminal actions. The third alternative is providing for a public prosecutor with additional provisions permitting the victim or his representative to participate actively in the prosecution. Under the third alternative the injured party may be permitted to institute a criminal action subsequent to a failure of the prosecutor to take action.[1]

The American jurisdictions have unanimously endorsed the principle that a crime is an offense against the peace and dignity of the governmental unit, rather than a personal affront against the individual victim. Following this principle, over half the states have created by constitutional provision the office of public prosecutor (known variously as prosecuting attorney, district attorney, county attorney, commonwealth attorney, county solicitor, and similar descriptive terms). The remaining states have created the office by statute.

Public prosecution is a unique American institution—a *sui generis*. The American colonies rejected the common law concept that prosecution was the responsibility and the right of private citizens, and provided the prosecutor as an alternative. It has been theorized that this action was primarily for the convenience of the colonists, although others believe it was for the purpose of diminishing the power of the attorney general and giving it to local officials.

Even today, private prosecution is the major method of instituting criminal proceedings in England. The Director of Public Prosecutions, a public prosecutor, acts only rarely, and then in cases where significant government or public interests exist. A majority of English prosecutions are initiated by police officers, who, depending on the seriousness or complexity of the case, either utilize police department personnel or employ a solicitor. The private citizen also possesses an independent right to initiate criminal actions.[2]

In the United States public prosecutors exist at the federal, state, and municipal level of government. The federal prosecutor is limited to cases relating to the specialized federal criminal statutes. The interest of the municipal attorney is normally limited to minor offenses and the violation of city ordinances. The state prosecutor, who is normally restricted to one county or one district (a group of counties), plays the most significant role in the administration of criminal justice since he processes the general felony and misdemeanor workload of the state. Subsequent material in this chapter will relate to the county prosecutor.

In a few jurisdictions a private citizen may begin a criminal action without the participation of the prosecutor (by going before a magistrate or a grand jury), and other jurisdictions permit private prosecution after the prosecutor refuses to act. For practical purposes, however, the prosecutor is vested with vast discretionary authority and virtually possesses the power of life or death over the fate of a criminal proceeding.

Duties of the Prosecutor

As previously indicated, many states have constitutional provisions relating to the office of prosecuting attorney. Most of these states, however, have deemed it advisable to permit the legislatures to prescribe powers, duties, and responsibility by statute. By way of illustration, the only specific constitutional provision (Article VII, Section 4) in Michigan concerning the prosecutor states: "There shall be elected for four year terms in each organized county . . . a prosecuting attorney, whose duties and powers shall be provided by law."

Legislatures have generally assigned prosecutors an impressive array of duties and provided them with broad grants of power. The prosecutor's most common functions relating to criminal justice are:

- Reviewing evidence prior to an arrest to determine if a citizen's observations or a police investigation constitutes sufficient grounds for arrest, and if so, recommending to the court that a warrant be issued, or if not, recommending to the citizen or officer that no formal charges be filed until additional evidence is obtained.
- Reviewing the evidence and circumstances of the case after an arrest has been made without a warrant to determine if adequate grounds for prosecution exist, and if so, filing formal charges, or if not, ordering the release of the accused.
- Determining what specific charge (and degree thereof) is to be filed against the accused.
- Initiating the formal accusation against the defendant.
- Taking action to terminate the case after it has been filed when in his judgment such action is appropriate.
- Negotiating with the defendant and his attorney for a recommended sentence or reduction of the original charge in exchange for a guilty plea (plea bargaining).
- Representing the state in various pretrial hearings and examinations.
- Recommending to the court the amount of bail for the release of the defendant.
- Representing the state in the trial of the case.
- Representing the state in cases which have been appealed. (In some jurisdictions this is done by the attorney general of the state.)
- Consulting with parole officials on cases pending before them.
- Presenting evidence to the grand jury and assisting it in its investigations and deliberations.
- Participating in training programs for local law enforcement officers.

Depending upon the jurisdiction, the prosecutor may also be responsible for rendering legal opinions for county officers, assisting in the collection of property taxes, drawing contracts for the county, and numerous similar civil law duties. Perhaps one reason for the many legislatively established responsibilities is that in many counties the prosecutor may be the only executive officer in the jurisdiction with legal training.

The prosecutor is responsible for making several key decisions in each case presented to him. Throughout the case, from early preparation through posttrial hearings, he possesses significant discretionary powers and enjoys near autonomy. Conceptually, such "free rein" authority is deemed beneficial to assure the integrity of the decision-making process. Conversely, however, in the wrong hands such power may tempt an official to participate in corrupt practices.

While courts are very reticent in acknowledging that the police officer possesses discretion, most courts recognize and approve of the prosecutor's discretion and indicate that it is well-founded in American jurisprudence. For instance, the Michigan Supreme Court indicated:

> The Prosecuting Attorney is a very responsible officer, selected by the people and vested with personal discretion, trusted to him as a minister of justice, and not as a mere legal attorney. . . . He is expected to be impartial in abstaining from prosecution, as well as in prosecuting, and to guard the real interest of public justice in favor of all concerned. This discretion is official and personal.[3]

The Federal Circuit Court of Appeals in a recent case examined the issue of prosecutorial discretion and held:

> The discretionary power of the attorney for the United States in determining whether a prosecution shall be commenced or maintained may well depend upon matters of policy wholly apart from any question of probable cause. . . . he is . . . an executive official . . . and it is as an officer of the executive department that he exercises a discretion as to whether or not there shall be a prosecution. . . . It follows, as an incident of the constitutional separation of powers, that the courts are not to interfere with the free exercise of the discretionary powers of the attorney of the United States in their control over criminal prosecution.[4]

The prosecutor possesses an immunity from civil liability for his official acts, even if such acts are done with malice or without just cause. This immunity rests upon a theory of public policy—the public interest dictates that such officials, because of the significance of their actions, should act freely and fearlessly in the discharge of their responsibilities.

Controls over Prosecutorial Discretion

Although rarely utilized, most states have procedures which may be implemented to control or remove a corrupt, incompetent, or unethical prosecutor.

Some states provide that the legislature either by impeachment action or a two-thirds vote may remove the prosecutor. Others provide for a removal by the governor after notice and hearing. Still others provide for removal by the state's highest court after petition. Local trials and ouster proceedings for improper conduct, as well as recall procedures by the voters, are available as remedies in some jurisdictions.

Some states grant broad powers to the attorney general to supervise at discretion any criminal prosecution. Where this power exists the attorney general can intercede in the case and substitute his judgment for that of the local prosecutor.

Some jurisdictions attempt to regulate prosecutorial discretion by requiring every felony case to be reviewed and indicted by a grand jury before it can be tried. In jurisdictions with this procedure, observers have indicated that under most circumstances the grand jury acts as the prosecutor's "rubber stamp."

Once the case has been initiated by the prosecutor and has reached the trial court, some states require a prosecutor desiring to terminate the case to file a motion requesting its dismissal and stating his reasons for such action. The court then possesses discretion to make the decision. The current practice in many jurisdictions is for the court to grant such requests automatically.

Where the conduct of the prosecutor is clearly unethical, a disbarment action may be requested through the Bar Association. This remedy is only practical in those states with a unified bar association which possesses disciplinary sanctions.

Informal control devices such as the news media, political parties, and organized vested interest groups may be able to exert influence on prosecutorial policy. This influence exists since such bodies have the capacity to present the issues to the voters, who in most states are ultimately responsible for the prosecutor's tenure in office. While such control mechanisms may function effectively in cases of blatant misconduct, experience indicates that it is doubtful that they have any significant impact on the day-to-day operations or case-by-case decisions. Such drastic action as removal from office seems unwarranted in cases involving issues over which reasonable men might disagree, and where bad faith or malice is not present. Only in the most unusual circumstances will any prosecutor find his discretion effectively challenged.

The Decision to Prosecute

The prosecuting attorney is confronted with three distinct types of situations which require him to decide whether or not criminal charges should be filed. A citizen may come directly to him and request that criminal action be taken against an individual. A police officer may present the results of an investigation in which no arrests have been made. A police officer may request that charges be instituted against an accused who has been arrested without a warrant.

Request by Citizen for Criminal Action

Numerous cases are presented directly to the prosecuting attorney by citizens. Businessmen and merchants frequently bring cases involving bad checks or business frauds to the prosecutor. Cases involving family desertion and nonsupport are referred by social service agencies. The participants in family disputes, neighborhood quarrels, landlord-tenant issues, and cases involving borderline conduct are often referred to the prosecutor by police officers who either feel they have no grounds for arrest or do not desire to take action because the nature of the relationship involves complex legal problems or a likelihood that prosecution will not result.

In many of these cases the prosecutor may act as mediator without involving the criminal process. His informal letter or phone call may result in restitution for the bad check, commencement of support payments, or resolution of other problems. In other cases he may refuse to prosecute and suggest that the citizen obtain a private attorney and explore the available civil remedies.

If he decides that the case merits prosecution, he prepares a criminal complaint which is signed by the citizen. The complaint is filed before a magistrate, a warrant is subsequently issued, and the police are directed to make the arrest.

Request by Police Officer Prior to Arrest

In a limited number of cases police officers may present the results of an investigation to the prosecutor before any arrest is made. Generally, such cases involve vice offenses in which probable cause is established as a result of a continuous investigation, e.g., gambling, prostitution, liquor violation, etc. Officers may also request a prosecutional review when the legal requirements are complex, such as obscenity and pornography cases; where there is doubt about the legality of evidence; or where the prosecutor's general policy has been not to prosecute certain types of cases.

If the prosecutor decides action is desirable the complaint is prepared, the warrant obtained, and the defendant arrested. Normally such review and action by the prosecutor not only involve his approval of a decision to arrest, but informally commit him to continue prosecution.

Request by Police Subsequent to Arrest Without Warrant

Since some 90 percent of arrests are made without a warrant, the decision to arrest in most cases is a unilateral one, made by the police officer observing the offense or possessing probable cause. However, the decision formally to charge an individual with the commission of a crime is far from being an independent decision of the police officer making the arrest.

After an individual is arrested he normally is conveyed to the police department and "booked." The booking process consists of recording the general facts of the arrest in a register, book, or blotter. Usually the individual's name, age, address, the crime for which he is arrested, the location of the arrest, and similar data are recorded. In some jurisdictions the prisoner may also be photographed ("mugged"), fingerprinted, and requested to provide information of a personal nature for a history or background sheet to be maintained as a part of his record. The extent to which the latter processes are followed generally depends upon the crime for which the individual is arrested.

Some police departments have established internal review procedures which must be followed before the arresting officer is permitted to request that a formal complaint be filed. In some cases a superior officer (sergeant, lieutenant, etc.) reviews with the arresting officer the circumstances leading to the arrest. In other cases, the matter may be referred to the detective unit for additional investigation ("follow-up"). In those cases requiring additional information to supplement the "probable cause" of the arresting officer, the suspect frequently is detained while the investigation is conducted. This detention should not be confused with the type condemned in the *McNabb-Mallory* cases. Those cases considered only the issue of the detention for the purpose of eliciting a confession. Of course, if the suspect is interrogated during this detention, *McNabb-Mallory* and their corollaries may apply to any statement obtained during this period.

After the review, the superior officer or detective approves or disapproves proceeding with prosecution. This may be based on many factors, such as the sufficiency of the evidence, the admissibility of the evidence, whether or not the suspect will function as an informant, whether the arrest was made for the purpose of prosecution, or for the safety of the arrestee (drunkenness) or general harrassment (prostitutes). The superior officer or detective reviewing the case applies the relatively objective standards of sufficiency and admissibility of the evidence or considers the beneficial aspect of having the suspect as an informer. In addition, in many cases, he will apply the same subjective tests that the arresting officer made in determining whether or not to proceed. Since the suspect has already been taken into custody, this review tends to be to his advantage, as it serves to some degree as a check on the arresting officer's judgment.

If a decision is made not to charge the suspect, he is released. This release is variously known as a "waiver," "discharge," or "floater." If a decision is made to request prosecution the arresting officer or the detective who made the supplementary investigation will normally request the prosecuting attorney to take appropriate action.

Factors Affecting the Decision to Prosecute

As a legal craftsman, the prosecutor's first concern will probably be with the sufficiency of the evidence. He will examine the evidence to determine if it does establish probable cause both for the arrest and for adequacy in surviving the preliminary examination. If he determines that it does, he has justification for filing the formal complaint and proceeding with the case. However, there are indications that most prosecutors require a higher standard of proof, and that even at this initial stage determine if the evidence will establish the "guilt beyond a reasonable doubt" required for conviction. On failing to find evidence necessary for ultimate convictions, many prosecutors will refuse to proceed.

A second factor receiving immediate attention is the admissibility of the evidence. The prosecutor should consider the police practices utilized in obtaining the evidence. If it was obtained under circumstances that will result in its exclusion at trial, the prosecutor is faced with a major ethical decision. If he views strongly his responsibility to function as a screening device to control illegal or questionable police practices, he can effectively do so by refusing to proceed upon the basis of illegally acquired evidence. On the other hand, some prosecutors might choose to weigh the possibility of the defendant pleading guilty to the charge and thus not forcing a confrontation with the exclusionary rule. Faced with this type of situation, the significance of prosecutorial discretion becomes apparent.

Many individuals who could be convicted upon available evidence are never charged. Others are charged with less serious offenses even though there is sufficient evidence to justify conviction of a higher offense. Numerous factors may influence a decision not to prosecute even though adequate evidence exists. There is general consensus throughout the nation that the resources of prosecutors' offices and courts are insufficient to prosecute fully the violation of every criminal statute. Limited resources may mandate the establishment of some type of priority system among potential cases to match work load with those resources. Cases which generally receive low priority are nonviolent crimes against property, such as forgery, embezzlement, "insufficient funds" and "no account" checks, fraud, and similar cases, where restitution of losses and private compromises can be negotiated between victim and accused.

Most prosecutors will probably consider the attitude of the judges and the community from which the jurors will be selected. Based upon experience, he will consider if these attitudes will result in an acquittal even though there is overwhelming evidence of guilt. Upon finding adverse sentiment he is faced with a decision of whether he should charge an individual for a crime when it is apparent he will be unable to obtain a conviction.

When an accused has violated a criminal statute requiring him to support his family adequately, most prosecutors will refuse to institute a criminal action if arrangements can be made for the accused to contribute to future support.

Prosecutors frequently refuse to take action where the offense is of a relatively minor nature and a filed criminal charge would do irreparable damage to the accused or his family. For instance, if a highly respected civic leader were apprehended for voyeurism, the prosecutor might take no action in exchange for an agreement that the accused would obtain psychiatric assistance.

Prosecutorial inaction may also occur when the victim of the crime might sustain more harm, embarrassment, or ridicule than the comparable benefit of obtaining a conviction. An example of this situation would be the trauma of a thirteen-year-old girl testifying in open court and undergoing extensive cross-examination concerning a statutory rape charge.

Normally, when the victim of the crime expressly states a desire not to prosecute or shows some reluctance, the prosecutor will abide by the victim's wishes and refrain from taking action. Even though the prosecutor could compel the attendance and testimony of the victim by subpoena, he normally will not except in those few cases where public interest in prosecution clearly overweighs the desires of the victim.

The prosecutor may choose alternatives to the criminal law to accomplish his purpose. He may choose to follow procedures for civil commitments for insane or sexual psychopathic accused. When an accused is currently under parole or probation he may seek its revocation rather than proceed on the new charge. When another jurisdiction has a charge pending and is actively seeking the accused for prosecution, the prosecutor having custody of the accused may yield to the other jurisdiction and not institute charges locally.

A prosecutor may agree to forego criminal charges against an individual who has agreed to testify for the state ("turn state's evidence"), or who will function as an informant. The rationale behind this action is that the greater good is accomplished by utilizing the accused to ferret out other illegal activities for prosecution.

Other factors of consideration might include a statute requiring a disproportionately severe punishment, the complainant having improper motives, or the statute in question having a history of prolonged nonenforcement within the community.

Conclusion

The prosecutor's decision to charge is a highly critical stage of the criminal justice process. His decisions to prosecute or to forego action establish him as a significant policymaker. He not only acts as a control device upon the enforcement policy established by local police administartors, but functions as a check and balance on the legislature as well. Even the courts, for the most part, are limited to the adjudication of those cases which he chooses to initiate. A competent individual in this position exercising his discretion to undertake prosecutions with responsible, ethical, and compassionate precision can contribute immeasurably to the quality of criminal justice. Conversely, an inept, irresponsible, or corrupt prosecutor can effectively prostitute the system and render it impotent.

Discussion Questions

1. The prosecutor possesses an immunity from civil liability for his official acts, even if such acts are done with malice or without just cause. Is such protection desirable?
2. In many cases the prosecutor may choose not to invoke the criminal process. He may personally act as mediator between parties (through letters, phone calls, or conferences); he may institute civil remedies in the name of the state; or recommend the use of civil law. In cases where there is a clear violation, is the prosecutor thwarting the purpose of the criminal law by such actions?
3. Assume the police have presented the prosecutor with overwhelming evidence of a suspect's guilt of a major crime. Assume also that the evidence was obtained through clearly illegal police tactics. Should the prosecutor institute criminal charges?
4. The position of prosecuting attorney in most states is an *elected* office. What implications may this have on the quality of individuals who occupy the office?

Chapter Ten

The Defense Attorney

With the aid of prime-time television programs and the creative minds of mystery writers, the career of the criminal defense attorney is popularly conceived as being glamorous and dramatic—the legal knight crusading for a cause, à la Perry Mason. This television image has been reenforced by the spectacular and widely publicized performances of highly successful defense lawyers such as F. Lee Bailey, Percy Foreman, Melvin Belli, and a few others. Despite its numerous challenges, purported excitement and romantic attractions—particularly in the mind of the public—the practice of criminal law has traditionally been avoided by most attorneys.

One factor accounting for attorneys' avoiding the practice of criminal law is that most individuals accused of crimes do not possess the resources to make the practice of criminal law financially rewarding. A 1966 economic survey of Missouri lawyers disclosed that only 6 percent derived a substantial portion of their income from criminal cases. Usually the criminal law practitioner was found to have been a member of the bar less than five years. Criminal lawyers (and attorneys who practice family law) worked longer hours and earned less money than lawyers in other fields.[1] A secondary consideration has been the legal profession's tendency to hold criminal lawyers in low esteem—in some cases, perhaps, assigning guilt by association and acquiescing in the use of such derogatory titles as "mouthpiece" and "shyster." The profession traditionally has distinguished between representing a corporation that breaks a contract and a criminal who breaks a safe. Law schools have historically treated criminal law in a cursory fashion in their curricula, usually offering one specialty course in the field.

The attitude that criminal law is "dirty work," and that the criminal lawyer is the "garbage man of the profession" has been undergoing a slow reversal in recent years. The role of the criminal lawyer is beginning to emerge as one having considerable social significance. Many law schools are placing increased emphasis on the teaching of criminal law and conducting relevant field research. Numerous bar associations and legal organizations have begun to focus on criminal justice problems and the federal government is funding defense service projects and research.

Right to Counsel in Federal Courts

At common law full representation by counsel was permitted only in misdemeanor cases. In felony and treason cases the interests of the accused were allegedly protected by the trial judge; therefore, no counsel was permitted except to argue points of law or to raise questions or collateral issues before the court. After 1698 full representation by counsel was permitted in treason cases, and in 1836 full representation by counsel was allowed in felony cases in England.

In America the Sixth Amendment to the Federal Constitution provides: "In all criminal prosecutions, the accused shall enjoy the right . . . to have the Assistance of Counsel for his defense." However, in the early cases this provision was interpreted as only entitling the accused to employ and utilize counsel and did not require the government to provide counsel for a defendant who was financially incapable of doing so.

In 1790, the Sixth Amendment right was supplemented by an Act of Congress requiring courts to assign counsel in capital cases for federal defendants.

In 1938 the Sixth Amendment provision was expanded by a Supreme Court interpretation (*Johnson* v. *Zerbst,* 304 U.S. 458, 58 S. Ct. 1019, 82 L. Ed. 1461) to require the appointment of counsel for indigent defendants in noncapital federal felony cases. Right to court-appointed counsel for indigent defendants in federal courts is a relatively recent right. For almost 150 years after adoption of the Sixth Amendment, an indigent federal defendant had no assurance of assistance of counsel. Since 1938, legislation and court decisions have provided counsel at all critical stages of the process for federal defendants.

Right to Counsel in State Courts

Most state constitutions contain right to counsel provisions similar to that found in the federal constitution. Early state interpretations of these provisions were that the defendant was entitled to counsel if he could independently employ one.

By 1931 all states provided that an indigent defendant was entitled to appointed counsel in capital cases. Thirty-four states provided counsel for indigents charged with felonies and twenty-eight states provided some degree of representation for indigent misdemeanants in certain types of cases. The prevailing practice at that time was to assign unpaid counsel who served in the capacity only as a public duty.[2]

The first significant state case involving right to counsel reviewed by the United States Supreme Court was *Powell* v. *Alabama* in 1932.[3] Seven defendants who had been sentenced to death after a trial in state court, alleged inadequate representation by counsel. The Court held:

> . . . in a capital case, where the defendant is unable to employ counsel, and is incapable adequately of making his own defense because of ignorance, feeblemindedness, illiteracy, or the like, it is the duty of the court, whether requested or not, to assign counsel for him as a necessary requisite of due process of law.

The *Powell* decision utilized the due process clause of the Fourteenth Amendment to impose upon the states the duty of effective representation only in capital cases where the defendant was in some way incapacitated. It was not until almost thirty years later that the indigent's right to counsel in capital cases was made absolute regardless of the circumstances.[4] However, the reasoning presented by Mr. Justice Sutherland's opinion in *Powell* became the rationale to be utilized extensively in subsequent cases. He wrote:

> The right to be heard would be, in many cases, of little avail if it did not comprehend the right to be heard by counsel. Even the intelligent and educated layman has small and sometimes *no* skill in the science of law. If charged with crime, he is incapable, generally, of determining for himself whether the indictment is good or bad. He is unfamiliar with the rules of evidence. Left without the aid of counsel he may be put on trial without a proper charge, and convicted upon improper evidence, or evidence irrelevant to the issue or otherwise inadmissible. He lacks both the skill and knowledge adequately to prepare his defense, even though he has a perfect one. He requires the guiding hand of counsel at every step in the preceding against him Without it, though he be not guilty, he faces the danger of conviction

> because he does not know how to establish his innocence. If that be true of men of intelligence, how much more true is it of the ignorant and illiterate, or those of feeble intellect.

In noncapital felony cases the United States Supreme Court took the position in 1942 in *Betts* v. *Brady*[5] that the Constitution did not guarantee every person charged with a serious crime in state court the right to assigned counsel regardless of the circumstances. State supported counsel for the indigent was not required as a matter of Fourteenth Amendment due process unless the special circumstances involved in the particular case shocked the "universal sense of justice" or were repugnant to "fundamental fairness."

A series of United States Supreme Court decisions from 1942 through 1962 consistently expanded the "special circumstances" under which an indigent defendant was entitled to appointed counsel to the point where the doctrine of *Betts* was virtually nullified. Then in 1963 in *Gideon* v. *Wainwright,* a unanimous Supreme Court extended the right to appointed counsel to all indigent state felony defendants and concluded that "any person haled into court who is too poor to hire a lawyer, cannot be assured a fair trial unless counsel is provided for him."[6]

In 1972 the Supreme Court, in *Argersinger* v. *Hamlin,* held that indigents accused of misdemeanors must be provided counsel if a jail term may be imposed.

Right to Counsel at Critical Stages

While the foregoing discussion has been related to the right of counsel at trial, it should be noted that the courts have also been concerned with providing counsel at virtually every critical stage of the criminal justice process. Critical stage, for this purpose, can be defined as any point within the process where the accused has been afforded a right which could be more effectively implemented with the aid and skills of a legal representative. Most cases have dealt with questions involving a defendant without adequate means being deprived of counsel because of his financial inadequacies. States now have the responsibility of providing counsel for the indigent defendant (unless he waives the right) at the following stages:

- During custodial interrogation by the police.
- During a "line-up" held by police for the purpose of permitting the identification of the accused by the victim or a witness.
- During preliminary examination.

- During arraignment.
- During trial.
- During sentencing.
- During appeal of conviction.
- During hearing on revocation of probation.

In addition, Supreme Court decisions have required states to defer expenses for other critical services necessary for an adequate defense. For instance, the state must provide a free transcript of the preliminary hearing, a free trial transcript for appeal, a free transcript of post conviction proceedings, and a waiver of normal filing fees in past conviction proceedings. Some states have extended this trend further by providing such additional considerations as a defendant in a forgery case has the right to the services of a questioned document examiner at state's expense and a defendant of foreign descent who cannot properly speak and/or understand the English language is entitled to a court appointed competent interpreter. The right to court-appointed counsel has also been extended to juveniles being processed through juvenile court, in spite of the fact that delinquency hearings had previously been viewed as noncriminal determinations.

Even in the light of the foregoing cases, a defendant may waive his right to counsel at any or all of these stages and represent himself throughout the entire process. To be valid, such waiver must be knowingly and intelligently made. When a defendant proceeds *pro se,* a heavy burden is placed upon the court to determine the competency of the waiver and to take special steps at appropriate times during the process to be sure the defendant is aware of alternative actions available to him.

Methods of Providing Counsel for Indigents

There are four basic methods for providing counsel for indigent defendants. Under the widely employed "assigned counsel system," the court may assign counsel on a rotating basis among practicing lawyers within the jurisdiction, or may utilize a special list of volunteers, many of whom are recent law school graduates who are seeking both the experience and the nominal fee. A second system involves the use of the "private defender"—a lawyer who is specifically employed by a private legal aid society, which is funded from local charitable contributions or by various foundations. The third approach is the establishment of an "Office of Public Defender." The public defender, salaried from public funds, serves as an institutionalized counterpart of the prosecuting attorney. In counties with such officials, the indigent defendant's case is automatically assigned to the public defender. The fourth method of providing defense services is the "mixed private-public system" which follows the organizational pattern of the public defender's office but is funded from both private and public sources. To provide additional personnel for the various systems, some states have instituted a legal internship program which permits selected senior law students to assist in the preparation, and sometimes the trial, of cases under the direct supervision of a licensed attorney. Defenders systems may also be supplemented by assigned counsel when workload or special circumstances necessitate such action.

It is unrealistic to advocate universally the use of one system over the others. The development of an optimum system of defense services in any community would require serious consideration of the community's socioeconomic conditions, the volume of indigent defendants, the available financial resources, and the number of local attorneys and the nature of their practices.

It is estimated that 60 percent of the individuals charged with felonies in the United States are financially unable to employ counsel. Other estimates are as high as 80 percent for particular jurisdictions. With the right of counsel expanding to include indigent defendants charged with misdemeanors, having competent attorneys available on a full-time basis has become a necessity. They are needed both to assure the defendant's rights and to provide a higher degree of efficiency in court management than exists now. The more logical solution to this problem is to develop under the supervision of the court a formalized defender system of a type most suited to the locale. Such a specialized defender system would assure higher competence and skill for the defendant, while making maximum use of available resources, whatever their form, i.e., tax funds, government or foundation grants, or services of legal interns. Such a formalized operation would assure availability of representation in the most efficient and economical manner.

The Role of the Defense Attorney

The adversary theory of trial is employed in the United States in both criminal and civil litigation. This theory makes the opposing parties responsible for presenting *their* witnesses, evidence, legal theories, and contentions in such a way that the triers of fact may be favorably persuaded to their viewpoint. Trial tactics and strategies are utilized to weaken the other side's position and make it appear ineptly fabricated and unbelievable. The legal gladiators employ such weapons as objections, cross-examination skills, and theatrical closing arguments to nullify the opponent's cases in the jury's eyes. In this environment it is indeed true that "the man who represents himself has a fool for a client." The *Gideon* case and its various companions have been predicated upon Mr. Justice Black's statement that "there can be no equal justice where the kind of trial a man gets depends on the amount of money that he has." The intent of judicial decisions involving indigent defendants, at least since 1963, has been to attempt to equalize the poor man's resources with those of the government by providing a competent counsel to champion his cause.

A recent study of the role of the career defense lawyer portrays him as an "agent-mediator."[7] His survival depends in great part on cultivating and maintaining effective rapport with the organizational functionaries—prosecutor, judge, and probation officer. The study indicated that, because of the nature of the system and the practicalities of his profession, the defense lawyer prefers not to litigate the case before a jury. He has a vested interest in limiting the scope of the case and the amount of time consumed in processing it. The study concludes that the defense attorney functions as a "double agent" between prosecutors-judges and the defendant, relying on mutual cooperation to result ultimately in a plea bargain. All parties (with the possible exception of the defendant) are interested in and anxious for an expeditious termination of the case. The career defense attorney is therefore viewed as part of the bureaucratic organization. His loyalty to that organization is rated as higher than his loyalty to an ephemeral defendant.

This same data, however, can be viewed from another perspective. The police determined the validity of the case at the time of the arrest and by subsequent investigation. The prosecutor screened the evidence early in the process. By the time the plea negotiation stage is reached the case has withstood at least minimal judicial review. In all probability there is significant evidence for conviction. The plea negotiation process is recognized as a proper and valid means of resolving the criminal case. The advantages to the state are obvious—certainty of conviction without the large expenditure of time and resources. There are also concomitant advantages to the defendant—the avoidance of the ordeal of trial and possible publicity; the failure of the court to hear all the adverse testimony that would be presented at trial; the certainty of negating the length of the sentence; and the increased opportunity for probation. In circumstances involving a sound prosecution case against the defendant, he can admit to his attorney his participation in the crime and the lack of a valid defense. The defense attorney (with the defendant's informed consent) has a responsibility to explore the possibility of a reasonable negotiated plea, subject always to the defendant's ultimate approval or disapproval. Conversely, if the evidence is weak and there is doubt that the prosecution could sustain its burden of proof, or there is a valid defense either in fact or law, the defendant can maintain his innocence to his attorney. The latter is obligated to forego negotiations and assert the appropriate defense.

The theoretical role of the defense attorney requires the use of evaluative skills, judgment, and discretion. In the early stages of the process, he should be concerned with evaluating the state's evidence, both as to sufficiency and admissibility and with conducting independent inquiries not only to verify the state's case but to obtain data for possible use in constructing a defense. He should then assume the role of advisor, counselor, and confidant as he presents to his client an evaluation of the prosecution's case and the alternative defenses available. Utilizing his professional judgment and experience he should calculate the probabilities of conviction or acquittal and, if warranted by the circumstances, the feasibility of plea bargaining. Based upon the data mitted and the attorney's advice, the defendant should direct the at-attorney's future course of action.

If plea bargaining is indicated, the attorney should then become the defendant's negotiator or an "agent-mediator" between the defendant and the state. As any mediator, he should deliver offers and counteroffers between the parties, always relying upon the defendant to make the final decision. If the defendant chooses not to become involved in plea negotiation or refuses the prosecutor's offer, the defense attorney should apply his skills as a courtroom advocate and prepare as adequate a legal defense as is possible under the circumstances. The defense attorney should never knowingly permit a defendant to plead guilty when the state's evidence is insufficient or inadmissible, or when the defendant maintains his innocence, unless he fully informs the court of the existence of these conditions and permits further inquiry by the court into the nature of the plea.

One may take the viewpoint that a defense attorney is a "double agent" with his loyalties divided between the legal institutions and his client, or one may visualize the defense attorney as a zealous guardian of the defendant's rights and interests. There are, no doubt, mercenary lawyers whose prime concern is the condition of their bank balance and their score on the golf course. They are matched by other attorneys whose altruism, dedication, and concern for an indigent defendant is beyond challenge. Regardless of one's evaluation of the defense attorney's role or his personal motivation, it seems indisputable that it is better to have even a mediocre to average lawyer—even one with an establishment orientation—shepherding the defendant through the legal labyrinths, than to leave him to develop his own defense while staring at the bare walls of his jail cell. While *Gideon* does not provide an iron-clad guarantee of superb and unexcelled representation, it does mean that a confused and poverty-stricken defendant no longer stands alone before the bench.

Discussion Questions

1. Why has the practice of criminal law been shunned by most attorneys? How could this be remedied?
2. Some critics of the *Gideon* doctrine have indicated that since the decision requires that the state provide counsel for the indigent defendant, there is no longer an adversary system with *State* v. *Defendant,* but in fact a *State v. State* situation. If this is so, is it compatible with the American concept of justice?
3. The right to state-provided counsel for indigents has been extended to all misdemeanors. What will be the consequences of such a move? Will they be desirable?
4. Compared to the prosecuting attorney, how much discretion does the defense attorney have?
5. What are the alternatives to the adversary system of criminal justice?

Chapter Eleven

Preliminary Proceedings: The Inferior Court and the Grand Jury

After a decision is made to prosecute the accused, a complaint is filed before a magistrate of an inferior court. Even though the inferior court has authority to try only misdemeanors, in most jurisdictions in practice it also has a responsibility of performing many of the pretrial processes in a felony case.

After the magistrate reviews the complaint and possibly takes testimony of witnesses, upon finding probable cause, an arrest warrant is issued. If the defendant is not in custody, the warrant commands his arrest. If the defendant is in custody, the warrant authorizes his detention pending initial appearance before the magistrate.

In some jurisdictions, when the defendant has not been taken into custody and the nature of the offense and other surrounding circumstances indicate that a summons would secure the presence of the defendant, the magistrate may elect to forego issuing a warrant in favor of the summons procedure. By following this method, police resources are conserved and the defendant is spared the embarrassment and inconvenience of an arrest.

Misdemeanor Cases: Initial Appearance and Summary Trial

A defendant is brought before the magistrate for initial appearance on a misdemeanor charge which is within the magistrate's authority to try. The complaint is read and explained, and the defendant is asked to enter a plea. If he pleads guilty, the magistrate may make inquiries of the defendant and others concerning the circumstances of the case, and then impose a fine, a limited jail sentence, or both.

If the defendant pleads not guilty, the magistrate may immediately conduct a summary trial. This procedure is frequently utilized when the arresting officer has brought the defendant before the court in a relatively simple case such as a minor traffic infraction or public drunkenness.

The defendant may indicate he does not desire to proceed to trial because he wishes to employ counsel or obtain witnesses or, in some jurisdictions, to demand a jury trial. The magistrate will then set a date for trial and fix bail or release the defendant without bail upon his promise to appear. This is the usual procedure when an individual who has received a summons ("traffic ticket," etc.) initially appears before the magistrate.

The minor misdemeanor case is normally disposed of with a minimum of paperwork and legal procedure. In most states the complaint and the warrant (or a summons which follows the complaint in general form) are the only legal documents formally prepared.

In an overwhelming number of cases, guilty pleas are entered. In many jurisdictions the only parties directly involved in the procedure are the defendant, the police officer, and the magistrate. Prosecutors appear only in those rare cases where a jury trial has been demanded, the defendant has employed counsel, the prosecutor's office has made a public pledge to prosecute actively certain types of cases (e.g., drunken driving), or there is a possibility of considerable controversy or publicity. In a limited number of jurisdictions where work load and resources permit, the prosecutor or an assistant may actively participate in these cases.

Felony Cases: Initial Appearance

When a defendant in a felony case is brought before the magistrate for the initial appearance, the magistrate informs him specifically of the charge by reading the complaint and explaining it to him. In some jurisdictions the defendant is provided with a copy of the complaint.

Since the magistrate does not have the authority to try the case, a plea is normally not accepted, and if one is tendered or accepted it is not considered binding. Rather than determining guilt or innocence at this stage, the magistrate is responsible for clearly and effectively advising the defendant of various rights and performing ministerial functions to expedite subsequent proceedings.

The magistrate should advise the defendant that he is not required to make a statement and that anything he says can be used against him.

If the defendant is unrepresented, his right to counsel is explained. Upon inquiry, if the magistrate finds that the defendant is financially unable to employ counsel, one is appointed at state expense, unless the defendant knowingly and intelligently waives this right.

The defendant's right to a preliminary examination and/or presentation of the case to the grand jury is explained. He is also advised of his prerogative to waive these rights and the implication of doing so. If the defendant desires to exercise his rights, the magistrate makes provisions for scheduling the subsequent proceedings in the immediate future. If the defendant knowingly and intelligently waives these rights, the magistrate may certify or transfer the case to the court with authority to try felony cases. (Made in the absence of counsel, such a waiver, if subsequently challenged, will probably be the subject of close judicial scrutiny.)

The magistrate establishes the amount of bail for the defendant's release or orders him released without bail. If bail is required, the magistrate orders the defendant to be committed to jail until it is submitted to the court.

The magistrate then explains to the defendant the general nature of the further action to be taken in his case, advises him of its approximate schedule, and responds to any reasonable question.

Initial Appearance and Setting Bail

The bail system requires that money or property be pledged to assure the defendant's appearance at a hearing, examination, or trial. It is based upon the assumption that the threat of imminent monetary loss deters the temptation to abscond.

The amount of bail is normally established at the time of the initial appearance before the magistrate. In certain types of cases, however, generally of a minor nature, police officers are permitted to accept bail under statutory provisions or court rules prior to the initial appearance. The defendant may be released on bail any time during the processing of the case, even after conviction pending appeal.

At common law the granting of bail was a relatively uncontrolled discretionary decision of the lower courts. In this country an overwhelming majority of jurisdictions includes liberal provisions for bail within its constitutions or statutes and thus establishes some degree of control on judicial discretion.

The right to bail is generally recognized in all but the most serious offenses (e.g., murder) and under circumstances where there is a clear showing that the public would be endangered by the defendant's release (e.g., treason). Under traditional theory, a defendant should not be forced to undergo lengthy detention or imprisonment unless he has been convicted. This right to freedom before conviction allows the defendant the opportunity of unhampered preparation of his defense and prevents the infliction of punishment by confinement prior to conviction.

This right to be released prior to trial depends, however, upon the defendant being able to assure the court that he will appear for the trial. The fact that the defendant is a local resident or property owner, is employed locally, maintains his family in the community, the offense is not serious, or similar circumstances might be sufficient for the judge to permit his release without bail. Nonetheless, there has been a tendency for courts to depend upon bail, the pledging of money or property.

Unfortunately, the bail system requires that the defendant have property or a friend who is willing to pledge property. In far too many cases, this requirement results in the man of property or prestige being released, while the indigent, charged with the same offense, languishes in jail awaiting trial.

Mayor John Lindsay recently indicated that when defendants could not make bail in New York County, the average time spent in detention awaiting trial in felony cases was 5.14 months and in misdemeanor cases 1.77 months. He further indicated that 43 percent of those individuals arrested in 1968 and held in detention for trial were held for over one year. After trial approximately half of these individuals were either found not guilty or sentenced to the amount of time they had already served and released.[1]

The President's Crime Commission documented similar shortcomings and inequities within the existing system. It reported in felony cases that in some jurisdictions an extremely high percentage of defendants were unable to make bail: Cook County, Illinois, 75 percent and Brown County, Kansas, 93 percent.[2]

When the federal Bail Reform Act of 1966 was signed into law, President Lyndon Johnson remarked that there were hundreds, perhaps thousands, of examples of hardship and cruelty provided by the bail system. He chose three examples to illustrate his contention:

> A man was jailed on a serious charge. . . . He could not afford bail and spent one hundred one days in jail until a hearing. Then the complainant admitted the charge was false.
>
> A man could not raise three hundred dollars bail. He spent fifty-four days in jail waiting trial for a traffic offense, for which he could have been sentenced to no more than five days.

A man spent two months in jail before being acquitted. In that period he lost his job and his car, and his family split up. He did not find another job for four months.[3]

Few people would argue that a defendant should be released without bail (or even admitted to bail) when this release would seriously jeopardize the safety of a specific individual or the public generally, or when the probability of the defendant fleeing the jurisdiction to avoid standing trial on a serious offense is extremely high. However, in many cases the present system does not make sophisticated discrimination between the potentially violent or transient individual and one who would be a substantially low risk. A standard amount of bail for each type of offense regardless of the defendant's circumstances is an easy method of avoiding inquiry into his background or an individual decision.

Within the past few years, some jurisdictions have been conducting research, operating pilot projects, providing legislative reforms, and generally attempting to establish alternative means of accomplishing the purpose of the bail system—assuring that the defendant will appear in court. Such projects include investigations and interviews to determine the defendant's employment history, his stability within the community, past criminal record, and other relevant information for presentation to the court for use in making its decision relating to bail. Some legislation has provided for conditional release without bail contingent upon the defendant's compliance with restrictions established by the court. In some jurisdictions more extensive use of summons by police officers has been encouraged both by legislation establishing the legal machinery and by police department policy.

The simple fact that an individual has been accused of committing a crime should not alone be sufficient to deprive him of his freedom pending trial. The fact that an accused has the ability to acquire financial resources should not be the prime criterion for his release. When there is relatively little risk in freeing a defendant without bail, in addition to the advantages afforded to the individual, such release permits the state to forego the expenditure of housing, feeding, clothing, and providing medical attention during a lengthy detention.

The trend today appears to be to seek alternatives to monetary bail and, insofar as possible, to make the defendant's poverty irrelevant to the issue of his release.

Procedures Following Initial Appearance

The felony defendant in most jurisdictions is entitled to a preliminary examination within a short time after his initial appearance.

Some jurisdictions merge the function of the initial appearance and the preliminary examination into one hearing. If this examination establishes probable cause to proceed to trial, the case will be (1) presented to the grand jury for action, or (2) transferred to the trial court by the prosecutor filing a formal accusation, known as an "information." The method to be used depends upon the constitutional and statutory requirements of the particular jurisdiction.

The federal government and approximately half the states require that most felony cases be submitted to a grand jury for review. In these jurisdictions the trial of the defendant may proceed only after the grand jury has issued an indictment, or the defendant has waived action by the grand jury. In these states the preliminary examination and the indictment are considered independent, and not sequential or contingent proceedings. A dismissal of the case at preliminary examination does not prohibit the prosecutor from subsequently submitting the case to the grand jury. Conversely, the immediate submission of the case to the grand jury for consideration does not deprive the defendant of the right to a preliminary examination, pending the grand jury's decision. However, once the grand jury has issued an indictment, the preliminary examination becomes unnecessary in most of these jurisdictions.

In twenty-two states the prosecutor has the option of submitting the case to the grand jury or, after a finding of probable cause at the preliminary examination, proceeding to the trial court by filing the information. In such jurisdictions, prosecutors have overwhelmingly chosen to utilize the information method rather than the grand jury.

The Preliminary Examination

The preliminary examination conducted by the magistrate functions basically as a screening device to determine if there is sufficient evidence to require the defendant to stand trial. The preliminary examination is not an inquiry to establish the defendant's guilt or innocence, but is a hearing designed to determine (1) if a crime has been committed, and (2) if the evidence establishes probable cause to believe the defendant committed it.

The state is required to produce witnesses, who testify under oath to establish its burden of proof. Since it is only necessary to establish the commission of the crime, and the probable guilt of the defendant, the state is not required to present all its witnesses, its entire case, or meet the burden of proving "guilt beyond a reasonable doubt" that will be required at trial.

The defendant has a right to be represented by counsel (court-appointed at state expense if he is indigent); to cross-examine state witnesses, and to call witnesses in his own behalf. The procedure utilized in conducting the hearing, although more informal, is similar to that employed at the trial. The preliminary examination frequently is officially recorded by a court reporter and transcripts are produced for subsequent use. Recorded testimony presented at a preliminary examination may, under proper conditions, be used at the trial to impeach a witness who makes inconsistent statements, to function as the testimony of a justifiably absent witness, and for similar purposes. Therefore, even if a defendant or his counsel is certain that the state can establish its burden of proof at the preliminary examination, it still may prove a tactical advantage to conduct the hearing. In its cross-examination the defense has the opportunity to explore the strength and weakness of the state's case.

If the state meets its burden of proof, the magistrate will issue a "bind over" order or certification. This action indicates that a preliminary examination has been held and, on the evidence presented there, he has concluded that a crime has been committed and that probable cause exists to believe the defendant committed it. This certification confers jurisdiction upon the trial court and authorizes the prosecutor to initiate action by information at that level. (In some jurisdictions, the order authorizes detention pending presentation of the case to the grand jury.)

If the state fails to meet its burden of proof, the magistrate will dismiss the complaint and order the release of the defendant. This dismissal does not necessarily terminate the case, nor preclude the prosecutor from filing another complaint on the same offense, since the defendant has not stood trial and has not been placed in jeopardy. Some states (especially those where the information option is available) have attempted, through judicial decision, to give the dismissal decision at the preliminary examination a degree of permanence. For instance, the Oklahoma Court of Criminal Appeals held in 1971:

> Dismissal at preliminary examination for lack of sufficient evidence to hold defendant for trial is a final and binding ruling and no subsequent refiling . . . shall be entertained unless the State makes an offer of additional evidence or proves other good cause to justify another preliminary examination. Additional evidence means that which was not known to the State at the time of the first preliminary.

Some defense attorneys insist upon a preliminary examination, not for the purpose of requiring the state to establish probable cause, but to utilize the hearing as a means of discovering and evaluating the state's evidence. In other circumstances defense attorneys are very eager to waive. Where the state's case is strong, defense counsel must weigh the possibilities of further alienating witnesses and court personnel, the possibility of increased adverse publicity, preserving, in permanent form, the state's evidence, the possibility of the prosecutor detecting weak points in his case and correcting them at trial, and similar disadvantages. Defense attorneys apparently view the preliminary examination more as a tactical device than as a significant part of due process. Similarly, in some jurisdictions the prosecutor may insist upon a preliminary examination, even though the defendant chooses to waive it. In such cases the prosecution is usually concerned with preserving the testimony of specific witnesses or with other purposes foreign to the main objective of the examination.

Indictment by Grand Jury

The grand jury is a common law institution with historical roots traceable at least to the twelfth century. In earlier times it wielded broad power and provided a significant vehicle for direct community involvement in local criminal justice. Today its powers, duties, and operational procedures are almost exclusively controlled by statute.

A grand jury is normally composed of sixteen to twenty-three citizens of the county or district, chosen to serve by a statutorily prescribed selection process, and summoned by a court with general jurisdiction over criminal cases.

Most cases are submitted to the grand jury by the prosecuting attorney after the defendant has been arrested and has appeared before a magistrate. In many cases the defendant may have been afforded a preliminary examination and been released on bail. In such cases the prosecutor prepares a "bill of indictment" against the defendant and presents it to the grand jury for consideration.

The bill of indictment will normally contain the name of the accused, the offense, with specific reference to the statute allegedly violated, the general details of the offense, including the time and place it allegedly occurred, and a list of witnesses who possess relevant evidence. The prosecutor will present witnesses to the grand jury to establish that a crime has been committed and that probable cause exists to believe that the defendant committed it.

The grand jury is responsible for determining if this probable cause is sufficient to require the defendant to stand trial. It is not concerned with determining whether the defendant is innocent or guilty, but rather with acting in the early stages of a case to prevent malicious or improvident prosecutions, and to avoid the expense of a public trial if the evidence is inadequate.

The prosecutor need not present his entire case or call all witnesses, so long as he satisfies the grand jury of the merits of proceeding to trial. Although designed as a screening device and a check on police and prosecutorial discretion, there are indications that the grand jury tends to function as a "rubber stamp." Its official pronouncements tend to reflect the opinions held by the prosecuting attorney.

Usually the affirmative votes of twelve grand jurors (one-half to two-thirds of the entire grand jury, depending upon its size) are sufficient to approve the prosecution of the case. When such approval is obtained, the foreman of the grand jury endorses the bill of indictment and forwards it to the trial court. Such action is commonly known as returning a "true bill," or "handing down an indictment." When the requisite number of affirmative votes is not obtained, the bill of indictment is endorsed as a "no bill" or "ignoramus," and the defendant is not ordered to trial. Such action will normally result in the release of the defendant, although in some jurisdictions it is not a bar to the prosecutor's resubmitting the case to another grand jury.

In some types of cases, the grand jury possesses investigatory powers. On occasion a grand jury is called to investigate particular incidents of official corruption, organized crime, or similar matters of public interest. In these cases, a prosecutor or other legal counsel may be assigned by the court to give legal advice, and police officers or other investigative personnel may be placed at the grand jury's disposal. In such cases, the grand jury possesses the power through the court to subpoena witnesses, require testimony, subject to the right against self-incrimination, grant immunity from prosecution in exchange for testimony, jail for contempt those witnesses who will not cooperate, and similar collateral investigative powers, depending upon the specific statutory provision of the jurisdiction. When functioning in this capacity, the grand jury is not an agency of review, but an accusatory body, concerned with ferreting out criminal activity.

Upon discovery of sufficient evidence of criminal activity while functioning in its accusatory capacity, the grand jury may return an indictment requiring the defendant to stand trial. (When the grand jury's findings are the result of its own investigation and not derived directly from evidence presented by the prosecutor or other officials, the formal accusation is technically called a "presentment" instead of an indictment. In most cases, the presentment serves the same purpose as the indictment.)

The proceedings of the grand jury are secret. The defendant or the subject of the inquiry has no right to be present or be represented by counsel. He has no right to appear and testify or require the grand jury to hear witness favorable to him. In this sense, the inquiry may be limited only to the evidence the prosecutor chooses to present or the witnesses the grand jury desires to call. Of course, these restrictions could be altered by legislation, but no such trend is presently apparent.

The grand jury and the preliminary examination generally perform the same function as related to defendants who have been arrested. The only basic distinction from the defendant's standpoint is his right to be represented by counsel, his right to confront and cross-examine witnesses, and his right to produce witnesses and evidence at the preliminary examination as opposed to the *ex parte* nature of the grand jury.

Conclusion

This chapter has outlined the general principles and procedures applicable to preliminary proceedings. However, it must be recognized that such procedures are provided by the constitution, statutes, and court rules of each jurisdiction and therefore may vary in shades or degrees as specifically applied in an individual state.

But regardless of specific applications, the primary purposes of the preliminary proceedings before the magistrate and the grand jury are to assure that the state is bringing the defendant to trial on probable cause, that the defendant's rights are properly secured, and that the cases proceed toward trial in an orderly due process fashion.

Discussion Questions

1. How may the inequities inherent in a bail-bond system be overcome in the local jurisdiction?
2. What significant philosophical distinctions exist between the preliminary examination method and the grand jury method of bringing the case before the trial court?
3. What would be the consequences of removing the veil of secrecy from grand jury proceedings?
4. What advantages may accrue to an accused as a result of the preliminary hearing?

Chapter Twelve

Preliminary Proceedings in the Trial Court

Following the return of the indictment or the filing of the information the defendant is arraigned before the court having jurisdiction over the offense.[1] The arraignment is a procedure requiring the defendant to appear before the court and answer the charge lodged against him.

The indictment or information is read or its contents substantially summarized for the defendant. A copy of the document is presented to him if he has not previously received one.

If the defendant appears without counsel he must be advised of his right to representation. The judge must further advise him that if he is indigent he is entitled to counsel at the government's expense. Unless the right to counsel is knowingly and intelligently waived, grave doubt will be cast upon the validity of subsequent proceedings. It is the judge's duty to make diligent inquiry to assure the defendant is fully informed concerning the consequences of such a waiver.

Normally, when the defendant is not represented by counsel and desires to employ one, the court will delay the arraignment a reasonable period of time to provide an opportunity for employment and consultation. This is also true in the case of a court-appointed attorney, or when the defendant does not desire representation but indicates a need for the delay.

Following the reading or summarization of the charging document (or subsequent to a delay to obtain counsel), the defendant is asked to enter a plea to the charge.

Pleas

Depending upon the statutory provisions of the jurisdiction, the defendant may enter a plea of guilty, not guilty, *nolo contendere,* former jeopardy, stand mute, or make a motion to invalidate the indictment or information.

If the defendant pleads guilty, the court may sentence him immediately or set a specific date for sentencing within the near future.

If the defendant pleads not guilty, he denies every material allegation contained in the accusation and requires the state to establish them beyond a reasonable doubt. After the entry of this plea the defendant may be asked if he desires to be tried by a jury or before a judge without a jury (in those jurisdictions which permit the defendant to waive jury trail). The court will then docket the case for trial.

Nolo Contendere

In approximately half the states and in the federal courts the defendant may enter a plea of *nolo contendere.* By the entry of this plea the defendant indicates that he is not guilty but has chosen not to contest the case and is uninterested in an adjudication of his guilt or innocence. If the acceptance of the plea is approved by the prosecutor and the judge, it has the same procedural effect as a guilty plea. The only major advantage of this plea is that it cannot be subsequently introduced into evidence in a civil case for damages to establish the defendant committed the act. For all other purposes, it is considered a conviction.

Standing Mute

The defendant may choose to stand mute and not enter a plea. When this occurs, the judge will enter a plea of not guilty and proceed accordingly. The only major advantage of standing mute is that in some jurisdictions the entry of a plea indicates that the defendant accepts the jurisdiction of the trial court. He thus waives any irregularities or defects which have occurred in the preliminary proceedings before the magistrate or grand jury. When the defendant stands mute, no such waiver occurs.

Former Jeopardy

A plea of former jeopardy is based upon the principle that a person cannot be tried twice for the same offense. Such a plea involves circumstances in which the defendant had been (1) formerly convicted of the same crime, (2) formerly acquitted of the same crime, or (3) subjected to trial-court action on the same crime which reached a stage where he was placed in jeopardy even though no verdict was obtained. For the purposes of this plea, jeopardy attaches when the trial jury is empaneled and sworn or in a trial without a jury when the first witness is sworn. If after that time the case is discontinued without valid cause or without defendant's approval before a verdict is obtained, the state may not reinstitute the action. However, the double jeopardy plea is invalid if the case is discontinued prior to jeopardy attaching; the jury is unable to agree upon a verdict ("hung jury"); an emergency arises such as illness of a juror or the judge or a fire in the courthouse; the defendant obtains a reversal of a guilty verdict on appeal; or similar circumstances.

Motions

After the indictment or information is filed, the defendant may utilize a number of motions in an attempt to obtain dismissal of the case or obtain assistance or tactical advantage in the preparation of his case. These motions may be filed prior to the time of arraignment, at the arraignment, or prior to trial. A motion is a request asking for a court determination concerning a right of the defendant, an error made by the prosecution, or consideration of circumstances requiring special relief.

Motions Directed Toward Dismissal of the Case

A number of motions may be filed in an attempt to obtain a dismissal of the case at the arraignment stage. Depending upon the jurisdiction they are variously known as the demurrer, motion to quash, or motion to set aside the indictment or information. These motions originated at common law and had narrowly defined and structured usage. The trend today is to abolish these specialized forms and to merge their functions in a motion simply labeled a "motion to dismiss."

Motions may challenge the legality of previous proceedings held in the lower court or before the grand jury. These motions request that the trial not proceed because of alleged irregularities. Such irregularities may include failure to endorse the names of witnesses upon the indictment or information, the presence of unauthorized individuals during grand jury deliberations, ignoring the statutory procedures for selecting and empanelling the grand jury, the information not signed by the prosecutor, and similar defects.

Motions may be directed at defects in the indictment or information challenging the technical sufficiency and language of the document. In effect, this motion takes the position that if every fact alleged in the document were true, it would still fail adequately to charge the commission of an offense by the defendant. This motion is applicable when an element of the offense is omitted in the charging document. Such omissions generally occur because of haste or the prosecutor's lack of experience, skill, or draftsmanship. On occasion a secretary's typographical error or omission of a critical line in the document may create the difficulty.

The defendant may challenge the jurisdiction of the court to try the case. This may occur when the crime is committed in a county outside the court's geographical boundaries, when the offense is a misdemeanor not triable in a general jurisdiction court, or when necessary prerequisites to the court jurisdiction (such as the preliminary examination) have not taken place.

The motion to dismiss may be predicated upon the expiration of the statute of limitations. State statutory provisions generally require that the prosecution for most felonies be undertaken within a period of from one to seven years, depending upon the jurisdiction and the seriousness of the crime. This motion is usually filed when the prosecutor fails to allege a specific date upon which the offense was committed.

Obviously, these motions are directed to the technical form of the process, rather than the substance or merits of the case. Most motions of this nature are regarded as dilatory tactics, concerned primarily with delaying the trial of the case. Under most circumstances, the judge will permit the prosecutor to amend the charging document or make insignificant changes to correct oversights. In the limited number of cases involving substantial infringements of the defendant's rights, such as failure to provide the defendant with a preliminary examination, the judge will return the case to the magistrate court for the rectification of the irregularity. In circumstances where the defendant can establish such defects as the expiration of the statute of limitations, the case is dismissed. However, relatively few cases are terminated using the vehicle of the motion to dismiss at the arraignment stage.

Motion to Suppress the State's Evidence

A motion to suppress the state's evidence may be filed prior to the time of trial, and frequently is filed during the arraignment or shortly thereafter. It may also be interposed during the trial to raise objection to the admission of evidence.

The motion alleges that evidence that the state plans to use at the trial was obtained unlawfully through the violation of the defendant's rights. Normally, this motion is filed in an attempt to exclude evidence obtained as a result of a search or wiretap, or to challenge the validity of a confession.

When the motion is filed prior to trial, the court normally conducts a hearing and allows the defense to present witnesses, including the police officers involved, to establish grounds for exclusion of the evidence. The state is permitted to cross-examine the defense witnesses and call its own witnesses. On conclusion of the hearing, the judge determines the admissibility of the questioned evidence. If he rules the evidence inadmissible, the prosecutor is placed in a position where he must determine if his case is sufficient to proceed to trial without the use of the excluded evidence. If he concludes it is not, he may ask the court to dismiss the case.

If the motion to suppress is presented during the trial as an objection to evidence the state has tendered for admission, the judge, outside the hearing of the jury, may conduct a similar hearing.

Motions for a Bill of Particulars

To be technically correct the indictment or information must contain, among other things, a statement of the act constituting the offense. The accusation must be certain and direct concerning the particular circumstances of the offense charged. It is possible for the accusation to meet these requirements and yet be drawn in such cryptic form or be so encrusted with legalese that the major issue is not clearly defined.

Under such circumstances a defendant may file a motion for a "bill of particulars." The bill of particulars is a supplementary document, prepared by the prosecutor, which presents more elaborate details of the charge. If, upon defendant's motion, the court, at its discretion, determines the bill is necessary to the effective preparation of the defense, it may order its preparation.

Normally the bill of particulars is viewed only as a means of obtaining clarification and details of the charge, and not a method for requiring the state to disclose its evidence or the legal theory and strategies upon which the case is based. However, the bill can play a very important role in aiding the development of the defense's case. For instance, if a defendant is charged with conspiracy it would be very important for the defense attorney to have the names of *all* the alleged conspirators rather than be surprised during the second day of trial by the testimony of a coconspirator of whom he was previously unaware. The same would be true in the case of a bookstore owner charged with possession of obscene material subsequent to confiscation of several different volumes. Without the bill he might not know which particular book was the subject of the charge.

Motion for Discovery of Evidence

A motion for discovery is a procedure whereby the defendant under some circumstances may be permitted prior to trial to examine certain evidence possessed by the prosecutor. At common law there were no provisions for discovery. In most jurisdictions today the defendant still has only limited rights to obtain pretrial disclosure of the prosecutor's case beyond that which is presented through the formal accusation, the bill of particulars, and the preliminary examination. The federal courts and a few state courts have liberalized the strict position of nondisclosure established by the early cases. They have endowed the judge with relatively broad discretionary power to order the prosecution to permit the defendant to examine specific evidence when such examination is shown to be necessary to the preparation of the defense's case. Such examination may extend to almost any physical evidence such as weapons, photographs, laboratory reports, or items seized in a search. Normally statements made by witnesses and notes and memoranda which are solely a work product of the prosecutor have been considered beyond the scope of discovery.

Because of the defendant's privilege against self-incrimination the prosecutor does not have a general right of discovery. However, depending upon the laws of the particular state, the prosecution may be entitled to notice of the defendant's intention to use alibi or insanity as a defense and may obtain the names of witnesses to be utilized for this purpose.

The arguments generally presented against discovery are that it provides the defendant or his counsel greater opportunity to (1) prepare perjurious testimony, (2) intimidate witnesses and informants, and (3) interfere prematurely with continuous police investigation collateral to the case. While recognizing these shortcomings, it appears that the clear trend toward more disclosure is being accepted. This trend is part of an attempt to eliminate manipulation and surprise during trial, and to promote the concept of the trial as a truth-seeking mechanism, rather than an arena for legal gladiators.

Motion for a Change of Venue or Judge

If it can be established that a fair and impartial trial cannot be obtained in the county in which the crime is committed, the defendant is entitled to have the trial removed to another county. This is accomplished by filing a "Motion for a Change of Venue." The court may hold a hearing and require proof of local prejudice. While the right is traditional for the defendant, the prosecution does not have this right in the absence of constitutional or statutory provisions. A "Motion for a Change of Judge" or a "recusation" may be utilized to request the assignment of another judge to try the case based upon the grounds of bias and prejudice or other disqualifying consideration.

Motion for Continuance

The court may grant a continuance, at its discretion, when valid reasons are presented by the defendant. Some of the more common reasons presented are the unavailability of an important witness, illness of the defendant, the need for more time to prepare the case adequately, or the recent discharge of the defendant's attorney.

Conclusion

The proceedings in the trial court prior to the actual trial of the case should be structured to provide the defendant with adequate information for an informed plea and a factual basis upon which he may prepare a defense. In addition, the proceedings should be concerned with assuring the defendant his constitutional rights and correcting any defects in previous proceedings, thereby avoiding the reversal of the case on appeal and the concomitant expenses of a retrial. Whenever possible the pretrial procedures should be designed to save time, expense, and talent through minimizing unnecessary bureaucratic repetition. Throughout the process, prime consideration should be given to accomplishing the pretrial proceedings' goal of paving the way for an efficient and effective trial in conformance with principles of due process.

Discussion Questions

1. What is the distinction between a plea of guilty and a plea of *nolo contendere*? Is the plea of *nolo contendere* philosophically incompatible with the American concept of justice in that it permits punishment of a defendant who maintains his innocence without requiring the state to produce evidence of guilt?
2. When does jeopardy attach? Should it attach earlier in the proceedings?
3. An early common law court stated that there was no principle to warrant a discovery procedure whereby the defendant could be permitted prior to trial to examine evidence possessed by the prosecution. The court concluded that such a procedure "would subvert the whole system of criminal law." Today, beyond the formal accusation, a defendant has only a limited right to disclosure of the prosecution case through a motion for discovery of evidence. What would be the consequences of permitting full disclosure of the states cases? Would this be desirable?
4. What protections do the preliminary proceedings in the trial court afford the accused?

Chapter Thirteen

Conviction Without Trial: The Guilty Plea

It is popularly believed that the determination of guilt or innocence occurs in the courtroom after lengthy deliberations of a jury following several days of testimony and dramatic closing arguments presented by able counsel. Such belief, no doubt prompted by television portrayals and newspaper reports of spectacular trials, assumes that the finding of guilt is a judicial process. In fact, considering the total volume of criminal cases, the judiciary plays a relative minor role in adjudicating guilt. Ninety percent of all convictions are obtained as a result of guilty pleas. In practice, the American system of criminal justice is predicated on the assumption that an overwhelming number of defendants will plead guilty.

Procedure for Entering a Guilty Plea

The procedure for pleading guilty in minor cases (such as traffic offenses and other ordinance violations) may amount to nothing more than the defendant signing a form which waives his right to appearance and mailing the court clerk a personal check to the amount of a predetermined schedule of fines. In other minor cases the defendant normally enters a plea on his initial appearance before a magistrate and receives a fine or jail sentence in a somewhat summary fashion.

In felony cases and in some serious misdemeanor cases, the plea occurs after initial appearance and preliminary examination, normally at the time of arraignment before the trial court. However, it may occur later on a special day docketed by the court for such purpose, during trial, or even after the case has been submitted to the jury, but before it has returned with a verdict.

The acceptance of the plea by the court is usually a very brief ritual at which the judge ascertains from the defendant if he is fully aware of the charge pending against him, the extent of punishment that may be assessed upon conviction, and the defenses available to such charge. The judge is also responsible for determining if the plea is entered freely, intelligently, and voluntarily.

Unlike hearings, examinations, or trials, when the defendant pleads guilty the state normally does not have a responsibility to present evidence. The judge is frequently unaware of the circumstances relating to the crime, except as they may be set out in the formalized legalese of the accusation. When the judge subsequently pronounces sentence, he tends to rely upon a presentencing report prepared by staff investigators assigned to the court (in those jurisdictions which have such personnel) or the recommendations of the prosecuting attorney. Some jurisdictions have formally provided for a postplea hearing during which evidence is presented to the court to establish the factual basis for the plea and to assure the voluntariness, accuracy, and basic fairness of the plea. In other jurisdictions some individual judges use informal devices (although not required by law to do so) to obtain the same result.

The court is not required to accept a guilty plea if it feels injustice will result. The normal remedy in a case where the defendant appears confused, ignorant of the proceedings, or incompetent to enter a plea is to appoint counsel for him, even though he may indicate that he does not desire one. In minor cases of this nature, acceptance of the plea is sometimes deferred until the defendant can employ counsel or has an opportunity to consult others and consider his course of action.

The Prosecutor's Role: Negotiating the Guilty Plea

Limited resources of prosecutors' offices and the courts, and the desirability of avoiding the time-consuming and expensive process of trial by jury have led to the universal practice of "plea bargaining." Plea bargaining consists of negotiations between the prosecutor, the accused, and the defense attorney to exchange prosecutorial concessions for a plea of guilty.

A significant number of guilty pleas in felony cases are obtained by this method. Prosecutors may make a broad array of promises in exchange for these pleas. The promises may include such actions as (1) recommendation of a specific sentence, (2) reduction of charges, (3) dismissal of other pending charges, (4) agreement not to charge the defendant with additional offenses for which adequate evidence is available, (5) recommendation of probation, and (6) similar recommendations.

This practice has been regarded by some as being somewhat unethical in that justice should not be the subject of barter and exchange. Despite such criticism, the courts have generally recognized that such practice, under proper conditions, constitutes lawful exercise of prosecutorial discretion. Since it is a discretionary process, it is subject to the same benefits and disadvantages as other discretionary decisions within the system—it may serve to individualize justice and promote fairness or it may be used arbitrarily and discriminatorily.

In practice, bargaining in some jurisdictions may occur as a standard practice, with a crowded hallway between courtrooms serving as an informal conference room while the court docket is being called. The prosecutor and the defense attorney may have little knowledge of the facts of the case or the background of the defendant, and may choose to consummate an agreement based more on personal relationships and tactical considerations than upon the equities of the case.

On the other hand, the negotiating process may occur in the reflective atmosphere of a legal office subsequent to a thorough investigation of all surrounding circumstances, including the defendant's background. And it may be primarily concerned with the best correctional alternatives available for the defendant.

In some jurisdictions, in certain types of cases definite customs and practices have developed. For instance, a defendant charged with armed robbery may almost automatically have the charge reduced to unarmed robbery by agreeing to plead guilty. The same practice may apply in reducing sale of narcotics to simple possession, felonious assault to simple assault, etc.

Where the guilty plea is obtained as a result of plea bargaining, the appellate courts tend to require that the promise be fulfilled or the defendant be provided the opportunity for trial.

The sentencing practices of courts seem to reinforce plea bargaining and generally encourage the entry of guilty pleas. With individual exceptions, most courts in practice render lighter punishment on guilty pleas than for conviction after trial on the same offense.[1] This practice may be predicated upon granting the defendant consideration for savings in time and expense. Other considerations may include that such admission is evidence of repentance and a step toward rehabilitation, as well as a willingness of the defendant to accept responsibility for his acts.

Conclusion

The prosecutor's plea negotiation concessions have frequently been the subject of criticism by local police agencies and other groups. Some equalitarians have been critical of the prosecutor's power to bargain where a man's liberty is at stake. Both sides have significant evidence to justify the elimination or strict control of this process. In a practical sense it must be acknowledged that the courts recognize and reenforce this facet of prosecutorial activity and rely upon it to effectively limit the courtroom work load. If every case were processed through trial, the present institutions and personnel would be almost totally incapacitated.

The process of plea negotiation will probably receive additional scrutiny in the future and may ultimately be subjected to more controls. In the light of present trends, it is doubtful that it will be significantly curtailed. Thus, criminal justice is, and no doubt will remain, a system wherein guilt determination is primarily an executive or administrative function—a system of justice without trial.

Discussion Questions

1. Should plea bargaining be abolished? What would be the consequences of its abolition?
2. Does plea bargaining detract from or enhance the prosecutor's duty "to see that justice is done"?
3. Should the judge be a party to plea bargaining?
4. Since sentencing practices of courts seem to reinforce plea bargaining by rendering lighter sentences on guilty pleas than for convictions after trial on the same offenses, does a defendant have a realistic choice other than plea bargaining if the state possesses substantial evidence of his guilt?

Chapter Fourteen

The Trial Jury and Its Selection

After the arraignment and necessary hearings on motions, the case is docketed for a specific trial date. When the case is called for trial, the first action is the selection of the jury.

The utilization of the jury system is firmly embedded in the American criminal procedure. This strong commitment to involve the lay citizen in the administration of criminal justice is guaranteed by provisions of most state constitutions and supplemented by legislative acts regarding procedural limitations and specifications. In all jurisdictions the jury is viewed as the instrumentality for determining the facts. It is given broad prerogatives in exercising its decision-making powers; it is allowed to deliberate in secret and reach a decision which it is not required to justify. The jury system is subjected to severe criticism by some authorities because it substitutes the judgment of a randomly selected group of inexperienced laymen for the professional judge. Other authorities proclaim that the jury is the strongest affirmation of a democratic system and the greatest bulwark of liberty man has yet devised. The merits and shortcomings of the system have been widely debated without resolution.

The jury is not as widely utilized as might be commonly believed. This is true for a number of reasons. First, trial by jury is not available to all criminal defendants as a matter of right in all situations. The right to a trial by jury, as provided by the Sixth Amendment to the federal Constitution and the various provisions of state constitutions, has generally been interpreted to mean the right as it stood at common law at the time the Constitution was adopted. Common law recognized a wide range of petty offenses which were tried summarily before a magistrate. However, individual states, through their respective criminal procedures, have considerable variation in permitting jury trials in minor offenses. For instance, Connecticut permits a jury trial only upon the charge of major crime, while Georgia permits the use of a jury on a wide range of minor criminal charges. In most states, the denial of a jury trial is not held as a violation of a substantive right where the defendant is charged with a "petty" offense punishable by less than six months confinement.

A second reason for the relatively low number of jury trials is that a vast majority of cases reach disposition before the trial stage through guilty pleas.

A third reason is the waiver of the right to a jury trial. In some states, the defendant has an option of waiving a jury trial and electing to have the case tried before a judge. Most states have placed some qualifications or restrictions upon an absolute freedom to waive the jury. Where waiver is permitted, the consent of the court and the prosecuting attorney may be required. Depending upon state law and local custom, waivers may occur in 75 percent of cases in some states (Wisconsin and Connecticut) and not occur at all in others.

The traditional jury in a felony case consists of twelve jurors, who must reach a unanimous decision concerning the defendant's guilt or innocence. In a recent case, the United States Supreme Court broke with seventy-two years of tradition and indicated that there was no constitutional requirement relating to twelve jurors and that a state could establish a procedure requiring a different number.[1] In misdemeanor cases, some states have expressly authorized smaller juries and have permitted a less than unanimous vote in misdemeanor cases, usually three-fourths of the jurors.

The Jury Panel

The state statutes or court rules will normally specify the procedure for selecting the jury panel (venire). Designated officials (jury commissioners, sheriff, clerk of the court, etc.) will compile a list of prospective jurors within the court's jurisdiction. This list will normally be taken from the voter registration lists or the tax rolls. The names will be listed individually on slips of papers or cards and placed in a jury wheel or device prior to the beginning of a term of court. The judge instructs the clerk or other official to select a jury panel. The size of the panel will vary according to the number of cases on the calendar, the amount of publicity that cases have received, and the anticipated difficulty in seating an unbiased jury. For normal operations the court may specify that fifty prospective jurors (veniremen) be called, but faced with a highly publicized, spectacular case it may request one hundred and fifty or more. The clerk randomly draws the prescribed number of names and prepares a court summons (venire facias) ordering them to appear for jury duty. The summonses are signed by the judge and served on the prospective jurors either by the sheriff or by certified mail. When there has been a material departure from the selection procedure established by statute, the entire jury panel may be challenged by a defendant prior to the final selection of a jury to try his case. If this challenge is sustained, the entire venire will be dismissed and a totally new panel drawn.

These procedures are established to provide, insofar as possible, a jury panel which is generally representative of the community. Courts, however, have recognized that the obtaining of an exact microcosm of the community by this procedure may be impossible. The United States Supreme Court resolved this problem by holding: "Neither the jury roll nor the venire need to be a perfect mirror of the community or accurately reflect the proportionate strength of every identifiable group."[2] The Court, however, made it equally clear that the Constitution bars conscious discrimination in jury selection by reason of race, national origin, religion, sex, or economic status.

The prospective jurors report at the time and place designated in the summons. The judge usually meets with the panel at this time and explains generally the operation of the court system and the responsibility and functions of jurors. He also explains that under law certain individuals are not qualified for service as jurors. Such *exclusions* may include persons who cannot read, write, or understand the English language; persons with unsoundness of mind or physical defect, such as deafness or blindness, which would render them incapable of performing the duties of a juror; individuals convicted of a felony; and such other deficiencies as enumerated by state statute or court rules. After explaining exclusions the judge asks those falling under these provisions to identify themselves. After inquiring concerning the conditions, and confirming them, the judge dismisses these prospective jurors from the panel. (In some jurisdictions much of this procedure is eliminated by early screening of the jurors through the use of a questionnaire which they receive with the summons.)

Following this, the judge explains that certain veniremen, because of special conditions, may not be required to serve as jurors, even though they possess proper qualifications. Individuals who fall under these special conditions may exercise an *exemption* and choose not to serve as jurors. Exemptions are specified by state statute or court rules. Some examples of exemption positions are: physicians, druggists, clergymen, dentists, newspaper men, hospital employees, veterinarians, radio announcers, college students, telephone employees, bank cashiers, public employees, and women with minor children in the home. The judge then inquires if any of the veniremen desires to exercise his option. If so, he may be excused from service. Upon establishing that jury service would constitute a hardship (even though the specified conditions are not enumerated in the statute), the judge may also excuse a prospective juror from service. The remaining members of the panel constitute the group from which the trial jury will be selected. There are many individuals who no doubt would make good jurors who choose to exercise the exemption for any number of reasons. Perhaps high among these reasons is that compensation for service as a juror is generally so low as to cause a financial hardship.

Prior to the first session of court, the clerk or bailiff prepares separate pieces of paper, each containing the name of a person retained as a venireman. The papers are folded as nearly alike as possible and deposited into a small box or other receptacle.

The clerk then calls the case, e.g., "The State of Missouri v. Jesse Outlaw." The judge inquires if the parties are ready to proceed. If so, the prosecutor and defense counsel so indicate. If a party is not ready to proceed, he must justify a delay and a postponement may be ordered. If the reason asserted is not adequate the judge will order the trial to proceed.

The judge instructs the clerk to draw the jury. The clerk draws twelve names from the receptacle containing names of qualified veniremen. The twelve selected are seated in the jury box.

Through a process known as the *voir dire* examination, the individual jurors are questioned to establish their qualifications for service in the particular case. Some ten states provide that the judge alone may conduct the examination. Eight states permit the attorneys alone to raise questions. In twenty-two states both the judge and the attorneys are permitted to question the prospective jurors. Ten states permit the judge, at his discretion, to conduct the *voir dire* or to permit the attorneys to do so.

Before the examination begins the jurors are placed under oath to answer truthfully questions concerning their qualification. The *voir dire* begins by either the judge, the prosecutor, or the defense attorney (depending on local law and custom) introducing the parties in the case and making general inquiries relating to jurors' qualifications. In a hypothetical case, for example, the prosecutor might begin by saying: "Ladies and gentlemen, this is the case of the State of Missouri versus Jesse Outlaw. I am Edward Counsel, the prosecuting attorney. The gentleman sitting at the far left of the table is Mr. Outlaw, the defendant. Sitting next to him is Mr. Mason, his defense attorney.

"I would like to make some general inquiries which may have a bearing on your sitting on the jury. I would certainly appreciate it if you will simply raise your hand if your response to any of my questions is 'yes.'

"Do any of you know, Mr. Outlaw, the defendant?

"Do any of you know Mr. Mason, the defense counsel?

"Has Mason ever represented any of your immediate family?

"The witnesses in this case will be Mr. Robert Grocer, owner of Bob's Supermarket at 12th and Spruce Street; Mr. William Clerk, a stockboy at the supermarket; Officers John Law and Aaron Copp of the local police department; and Miss Wanda Truelove, a student at the local university. Are any of you acquainted with any of these witnesses?"

After completing such general exploratory questions, counsel may ask questions of a specific juror relating to his qualifications. As an example of specific examination, the following material has been extracted from an Oklahoma Court of Criminal Appeals opinion:[3]

Defense Attorney: ". . . Mr. Smith, I would like to start with you now and ask you some individual questions which will be on your qualifications to sit as a juror. The complaining witness in this case is a fifteen-year-old girl by the name of Jane Roe, and she, through the county attorney's information, alleges that John Doe raped her. Based upon this charge or his information, and as I have explained to you, the county attorney has filed this charge and we are today defending John Doe. Do you believe, Mr. Smith, that he is entitled to make every reasonable effort to defend himself?"

Prospective Juror: "Yes, sir."

Defense Attorney: "Do you believe that when one person makes a charge against another that the person who is accused has a right to make an investigation into the background of the individual who has made these charges against him?"

Prospective Juror: "I think so."

Defense Attorney: "You think so?"

Prospective Juror: (Nods head.)

Defense Attorney: "Well, now then, do you think there is anything wrong with me as the lawyer for this boy or for the people working for me, I having accepted as a lawyer employment in this case, going out to talk to people who have known this fifteen-year-old girl, the complaining witness, in an effort to find out what kind of person she

is or was at the time of the alleged crime? Do you see anything wrong with it?"
Prospective Juror: "I don't really think so."

* * *

Defense Attorney: "Now then, even though the complaining witness is a fifteen-year-old girl in this case, do you believe and are you satisfied that this boy can question her credibility without your thinking he is taking unfair advantage of her?"
Prospective Juror: "I think so."

* * *

Defense Attorney: "And, so you have no quarrel with the boy's right to establish by competent evidence that what this girl says is untrue if he can so establish that?"
Prospective Juror: "I think that is right."
Defense Attorney: "All right, you do not feel then at this time that a fifteen-year-old girl can only tell the truth, that is, she is not capable of telling anything but the truth. You don't feel at this time that just because she is a fifteen-year-old girl she is not capable of telling anything but the truth?"
Prospective Juror: "No."
Defense Attorney: "Now then, I must explain to you that the very nature of this case is going to require considerable in the way of testimony about sex. . . . I anticipate that on occasion the testimony is going to border on the sordid and you may or may not, as I anticipate, hear four-letter words used from the witness stand and possibly by the lawyers in eliciting testimony from the witness stand. Would this in any way shock your conscience to the effect that you think it might interfere with your deliberations in this case?"
Prospective Juror: "I don't think so."

* * *

Defense Attorney: "I'll anticipate that the complaining witness will take the witness stand and that I will cross-examine her at length and I may have to ask her questions on cross-examination that I won't even discuss in the presence of my daughter, but it will be in an attempt to put before you the facts in this case. Are you going to take offense if I ask the complaining witness—I am a forty-four year old and this is a fifteen-year-old girl—things that would ordinarily be offensive, are you going to hold it against me or my client? You would not be offended?"
Prospective Juror: "I think anything permitted by the court would be all right with me."

* * *

Defense Attorney: ". . . you know a man is presumed innocent until

he is proven guilty beyond a reasonable doubt, is that correct?"
Prospective Juror: "Yes, sir."
Defense Attorney: "Do you also realize, Mr. Smith, that you must give the defendant, John Doe, the benefit of this presumption of innocence without any mental reservations whatsoever?"
Prospective Juror: "I think so."
Defense Attorney: "This is what is required, he is presumed innocent?"
Prospective Juror: "Yeah."
Defense Attorney: "And if you are permitted to remain on this jury, you must presume him innocent without any mental reservation whatsoever?"
Prospective Juror: "Yes, sir."

* * *

Defense Attorney: "Now then, Mr. Smith, do I have your promise that you will give this defendant, John Doe, the full benefit of the presumption of innocence?"
Prospective Juror: "Yes, sir."

* * *

Defense Attorney: "Now then, the Court will instruct you that the prosecution must prove every element of this crime beyond a reasonable doubt and he will tell you what elements are contained in the charge that is filed and they must prove every single solitary element of the crime beyond a reasonable doubt. Now then, if they do not establish beyond a reasonable doubt every ingredient to your satisfaction will you acquit him?"
Prospective Juror: "Yes, sir, if I don't get the doubt out of my mind."

* * *

Defense Attorney: "This is the charge that has been brought against the defendant, John Doe, that he '. . . did then and there wilfully, unlawfully, wrongfully, and feloniously, and by means of force overcome the resistance and by means of threats of immediate injury and great bodily harm, accompanied by apparent power of execution, and preventing resistance by then and there striking, beating, bruising and maltreating and holding one Jane Roe, a female of the age of fifteen years, and did then and there have and hold sexual intercourse with the said Jane Roe, a female of the age of fifteen, and not the wife of the said defendants, or any of them, and the said defendants being male persons under the age of eighteen years—and said act of sexual intercourse being accomplished by said defendants after having by force overcome the resistance of the said Jane Roe, and without her consent and against her will.' They must establish beyond a reasonable doubt, Mr. Smith, every single element of the charge. This is what I am talking about,

Mr. Smith, that the ingredients of the elements of the crime must be proven each and every one of them and the Court will instruct you as to what the ingredients or what the elements are and you will then require them to prove every single one of them before you will convict John Doe?"

Prospective Juror: "Well, you mean that we have to stay until we know every bruise and everything?"

Defense Attorney: "No, no. He will instruct you as to the ingredients of that crime and what must be proven before it can then constitute a crime but each and every one of these things has to be proven beyond a reasonable doubt. Not just a part of it, that is the point that I am trying to get over to you. If they just prove part of it and they don't prove the other or some reasonable doubt is existing in your mind or the others, then you must vote to acquit him and you would have no hesitation in doing so?"

Prospective Juror: "I don't think so."

* * *

Defense Attorney: "All right, now then, knowing that he (the defendant) is not bound to explain his side of the case, that he is not bound to satisfy you of his innocence, you would not, would you, Mr. Smith, consider that my client's failure to testify would be an indication of guilt, would you?"

Prospective Juror: "As far as guilt or innocence, yes."

* * *

Defense Attorney: "Have you heard, seen, or read any purported facts that this boy committed an act of sodomy?"

Prospective Juror: "Yeah, I wouldn't say exactly, actually I haven't been keeping that close of a touch. I know that I read of it."

Defense Attorney: "Does this fact that you have read this now affect you so that you might have some impression or opinion about the purported facts in this case or about the merits of this case?"

Prospective Juror: "I don't think it has. I haven't thought about it until you mentioned it."

* * *

Defense Attorney: "All right, sir, knowing what you know about this case as it has been brought out by my questioning here, would you be satisfied to be tried by a jury or a juror having your frame of mind?"

Prospective Juror: "That is what I am trying to do too, put myself over there."

Defense Attorney: "You would be satisfied if you were over there with a juror in your frame of mind?"

Prospective Juror: "Yes, sir."

* * *

Defense Attorney: "Mr. Smith, one last question, as we come into the Court today, does this boy have any strikes against him now as far as you are concerned?"
Prospective Juror: "I don't think so."

If, during the questioning, a prospective juror's answers indicate that he has sufficient knowledge, attitudes, opinions, or relationships which clearly indicate he would be biased and prejudiced in the case, toward either party, counsel may challenge the juror for cause. In some states grounds for *challenge for cause* are established by statute. For example, Oklahoma state statutes provide that grounds exist for challenge for cause when a juror has actual or implied bias.[4] Actual bias is "the existence of a state of mind on the part of the juror, in reference to the case, or to either party, which satisfies the court, in the exercise of a sound discretion, that he cannot try the issue impartially, without prejudice to the substantial rights of the party challenging." The statutes further provide (22 Okla. Sta. 660):

> A challenge may be taken for all or any of the following causes: . . . consanguinity or affinity [related by blood or marriage] within the fourth degree, inclusive, to the person alleged to be injured by the offense charged or on whose complaint the prosecution was instituted, or to the defendant. . . . Standing in the relation of guardian and ward, attorney and client, master and servant, or landlord and tenant, or being a member of the family of the defendant, or of the person alleged to be injured by the offense charged, or on whose complaint the prosecution was instituted, or in his employment or wages. . . . Being a party adverse to the defendant in a civil action, or having complained against, or accused by him in a criminal prosecution. . . . Having served on the grand jury which found the indictment, or on a coroner's jury which inquired into the death of a person whose death is the subject of the prosecution. . . . Having served on a trial jury which has tried another person for the offense charged. . . . Having been one of the jury formerly sworn to try the (case) and whose verdict was set aside, or which was discharged without a verdict, after the cause was submitted to it. . . . Having served as a juror in a civil action brought against the defendant for the act charged as an offense.

The counsel directs the challenge for cause to the judge. The judge then makes a ruling concerning the challenge. The judge may question the juror further if he has insufficient information upon which to base a decision. If the judge finds sufficient evidence to warrant dismissal, the juror will be excused and the clerk will draw another juror. Questioning will continue until the counsel who initiated the *voir dire* has no more reason to challenge any of the jurors for cause.

He then turns the examination to the opposing counsel who follows the same procedure. This process continues until neither attorney can find cause to challenge any of the prospective jurors.

Neither the defendant nor the state is entitled to have jurors with completely blank minds. The courts recognize that many jurors may have some knowledge of the offense obtained primarily through the mass media. All that is required is that the jurors have no fixed opinion which will prevent them from rendering a fair and impartial verdict, based upon evidence admitted in the trial, and the law as presented to them by the judge.

After twelve jurors have been tentatively accepted counsel may then exercise *preemptory challenges.* Utilizing a preemptory challenge counsel may excuse a juror without stating any cause whatsoever. The number of preemptory challenges available to each side are regulated by statute or court rule. For instance, in a felony case each side may be permitted ten preemptory challenges, and twenty in a capital case. Each time a preemptory challenge is exercised, the clerk draws a new juror, who is then subjected to questioning to determine if a challenge for cause applies to him. After both counsel have accepted the new juror for cause, other preemptory challenges may be exercised. In this fashion the process continues until all challenges are exhausted or waived. The twelve individuals remaining constitute the jury for the case.

Some states permit the selection of alternate jurors. If one of the principal jurors becomes ill or an emergency arises in his family, etc., he may be released and an alternate juror substituted. Otherwise, the trial would be jeopardized and, unless all parties agreed to proceed, would have to be started over with a totally new jury. There may be from one to four alternates depending on the state procedure or the custom of the court. The alternate jurors sit with the principal jurors during the presentation of the case, but are dismissed prior to the jury retiring to deliberate the verdict, except in a few jurisdictions which permit substitution any time prior to verdict.

When the principal and alternate jurors are selected the jury is sworn. After being placed under oath, the jurors repeat a statement similar to the following: "I do solemnly swear that I shall well and truly try, and true deliverance make, between the people of this state and the defendant in this case, whom I shall have in charge, according to the evidence and the laws of this state; so help me God."

It is not unusual for the jury selection process in a routine case to take several hours. In highly publicized cases the *voir dire* examination may take several days and in some cases weeks. The time expended by this process may vary greatly, depending on the nature of the case, the nature of the community, the amount of control exerted by the judge, and the personalities and trial tactics of the lawyers. Many successful attorneys have little faith in the lengthy *voir dire* procedures and practically accept the first jurors drawn. Other, equally successful, lawyers firmly believe that jurors should be selected with extreme care to assure attitudes compatible with their views of the case. The proponents of the lengthy *voir dire* indicate that beyond the advantages of obtaining an unbiased jury, it may be utilized to condition jurors for an unfavorable aspect of the case, to give them a background of legal terminology to be used in the case, and generally to highlight the elements of law and facts which are most favorable to their case.

Prosecutors' offices and defense attorneys may maintain the voting record of jurors in previous cases or have general background investigations conducted on members of the jury panel prior to the term of court. This advance knowledge may serve to reduce the selection process. In small counties, the attorneys and parties may be personally acquainted with many of the jurors and their background, which greatly simplifies the process.

Conclusion

Even though only a relatively small percentage of total criminal cases is adjudicated by juries, the right to a trial by jury should be recognized as a significant constitutional guarantee. The jury, composed of lay citizens, may serve as an effective check and balance upon official discretion, especially when the crime charged is one with political overtones or one in which community sentiment opposes official policy. Although in the context of the total system the jury may not exert a high degree of influence, in specific types of cases it may have tremendous impact.

Discussion Questions

1. Can a jury (or a jury panel) ever be generally representative of the community?
2. Does the exemption procedure inhibit the acquisition of a representative jury panel? What would be the consequences of mandatory jury service by all qualified citizens?
3. What actual purpose does the peremptory challenge serve? Is this in the interest of justice?
4. The *voir dire* examination in the case of Richard Speck, accused murderer of eight student nurses in Chicago, consumed twenty-seven days and six hundred and ten prospective jurors before the jury was finally empaneled. Is there an alternative to this costly process?

Chapter Fifteen

The Trial

The procedures utilized by trial courts are variously controlled by statutes passed by the legislature, court rules adopted by the highest court of the state, provisions of the state constitution, mandates of the federal Constitution as interpreted by the United States Supreme Court, local tradition and custom, and—in discretionary matters—by the personal preferences of the trial judge. Even with these many variables, court procedures for the most part conform to established patterns. This chapter will emphasize those characteristics that tend to emerge in the trial processes of most jurisdictions.

Public Trial

The Sixth Amendment to the Constitution provides that the defendant in a criminal prosecution has a right to a "public trial." With the exception of juvenile proceedings, and in a few jurisdictions where testimony of a sexual nature might "infect" the community morals, the general citizenry is admitted to criminal trials to the extent of available seating capacity. Even those states which permit exclusion of the public because of the sordid nature of the testimony have representatives of the press in attendance.

Presence of the Defendant

The defendant has a constitutional right to be present in the courtroom during every stage of the proceedings from arraignment through sentencing. This right takes on added significance in the context of current events and the tactical disruptions of courtroom proceedings by politically oriented defendants. Although the defendant's right to be present has long been recognized as fundamental, there is historical precedent that the accused may lose this right either by consent or through misconduct. A 1970 United States Supreme Court case clearly indicates that, under certain conditions, the accused may be tried *in absentia.* The Court held:

> . . . a defendant can lose his right to be present at trial if, after he has been warned by the judge that he will be removed if he continues his disruptive behavior, he nevertheless insists on conducting himself in a manner so disorderly, disruptive, and disrespectful of the court that his trial cannot be carried on with him in the courtroom. Once lost, the right to be present can, of course, be reclaimed as soon as the defendant is willing to conduct himself consistently with the decorum and respect inherent in the concept of courts and judicial proceedings.[1]

The opinion indicated that other permissible alternatives were to (1) "bind and gag him, thereby keeping him present," or (2) "cite him for contempt."

Opening Statements

After the jury has been impaneled the indictment or information is usually read. The prosecutor then makes his opening statement. The purpose of this statement is to inform the jury of the general nature of the case, the facts as the prosecution views them, and the significance of witnesses and physical evidence that will be presented to prove the alleged facts. The utility of the opening statement is that it outlines for the jurors, who are untrained in legal procedures and criminal investigation, the general objectives of the state's case and the methodology that the prosecutor will utilize. In theory, such early explanation assists the jurors in avoiding confusion, and in more complex cases, getting hopelessly lost in the labyrinth of testimony.

The opening statement must be restricted to the specifics of the case being tried. It is improper for the prosecutor to raise collateral matters which tend to prejudice the jury. The prosecutor must not make statements or allegations that he knows he cannot prove. Normally, however, reversible error cannot be committed during this presentation unless the prosecutor acts in bad faith with knowledge that his clearly prejudicial comment cannot be supported by subsequent testimony. The prosecutor must avoid argumentation or attempts at persuasion during the opening statement, and must confine his comments to the presentation of information.

Many jurisdictions regard the prosecutor's opening statement as a convenient and traditional method of introducing the case, but permit the prosecutor to waive the statement if he chooses. Some states, however, compel the prosecutor to make an opening statement and his failure to do so may result in the reversal of a conviction.

After the prosecutor's opening statement is concluded, the defense attorney may make an opening statement, or he may request permission to defer or reserve the statement until the prosecution's case has been concluded. If the defendant chooses, he may waive the opening statement. The almost universal effect of such a waiver is well stated in a recent Illinois case, which held:

> The purpose of an opening statement on behalf of a defendant is to apprise the jury of the nature of the defense and the evidence that is to be offered to sustain it. Since the opening statement is not evidence . . . it bears no relationship to the merits of any defense . . . and a waiver of the right to make that statement cannot raise any adverse inference against the defendant.[2]

The State's Case

After the opening statement the prosecution must present its proof by calling its witnesses.

The Sixth Amendment to the Constitution provides that "in all criminal prosecutions, the accused shall enjoy the right to . . . be confronted with the witnesses against him. . . ." Virtually all courts agree that confrontation, and such collateral aspects of it as cross-examination, are an essential, fundamental requirement of a fair trial and due process.

The courts, and especially the United States Supreme Court, have been giving increased attention to this area of due process in recent years. Recently, a conviction was reversed because a police informant testifying against the defendant refused to disclose his true name and address (with the approval of the trial judge), and thus, said the Supreme Court, deprived the defendant of his right to confrontation.[3] Some minor exceptions to direct confrontation at trial exist—for instance, the *bona fide* unavailability of a witness who gave recorded testimony under oath and subjected to legitimate cross-examination by the defense at a previous judicial proceeding in the same case. Constitutionally, the state's case must depend directly upon the testimony of its witnesses appearing in the public courtroom and disclosing their true identity.

The state's first witness is called after opening statements are concluded. The witness is sworn to tell the truth or make an affirmation to do so. The witness' responsibility is to give testimony relating directly to what he perceived through the use of his senses—not opinions, conclusions or speculations. The only exception is that a qualified expert may offer opinions and conclusions where the subject of the testimony is in his area of expertise.

The witness' testimony is acceptable only in response to questions by the prosecutor, the defense attorney, and on occasion, the judge. Some states permit jurors to submit questions to the witness through the judge, with his approval, but this practice is generally discouraged and rarely occurs. Witnesses are required to respond directly to the question asked, and attempts to avoid the direct thrust of the question or to volunteer additional information beyond the question's scope are strongly discouraged. The basic reason for requiring direct responsiveness is that a witness, if given freedom to do so, might blurt out material which is legally objectionable, and if highly prejudicial might constitute reversible error. The procedural restrictions upon the methods of receiving testimony are designed, insofar as possible, to assure that objectionable matter is not received by the jury.

If physical evidence is to be introduced, there must be a witness to identify it, testify to its relevancy, establish that it is in substantially the same condition as at the time it was obtained (or adequately justify why it is not), show there was no opportunity for anyone to tamper with it ("chain of custody"), and that it was not obtained in violation of the defendant's constitutional rights (if challenged by the defense). Physical evidence is introduced during the course of regular testimony, subject to the judge's approval as to admissibility.

The prosecutor begins the presentation of evidence by the direct examination of the first witness. In response to the prosecutor's questions the witness relates his information about the case. Upon the prosecutor's completion of direct examination, the defense may conduct a cross-examination of the witness. With this he attempts to clarify or enlarge upon the testimony from the defense standpoint and, on occasion, to impeach the creditability of the witness by attempting to discover any bias, prejudice, or interest. Upon the completion of cross-examination, the prosecutor may conduct a redirect examination, limited to those matters emphasized during the cross-examination. Following this, the defense attorney may conduct a recross-examination. Additional alternative examinations may be conducted by the attorneys but they are generally limited in nature and scope to those matters related during the immediately preceding examination. After the testimony of the first witness, the prosecutor calls subsequent witnesses, who undergo the same process.

When the testimony of the state's final witness is concluded, the prosecutor announces that the state rests its case.

Motion for Acquittal

At the close of the state's case, the defendant may enter a motion for a judgment of acquittal. Such motion challenges the sufficiency of the evidence to sustain a conviction and asks the court to rule, as a matter of law, that the state has not met its burden of proof.

Through the testimony of its witnesses the state is required to establish that a crime has been committed. The state must have submitted evidence relating to each technical element or part of the crime. In addition, the state is required to establish the defendant's guilt beyond a reasonable doubt. Although there are numerous commentaries regarding what quantum of evidence is necessary to meet this burden, most jurisdictions embrace the general rule that, if the evidence leads to no other logical conclusion than the guilt of the defendant, there is sufficient evidence to convict. Since the defendant is presumed innocent until his guilt is clearly established, if the defense can show two logical conclusions from the evidence—one that the defendant committed the crime and the second that he did not— reasonable doubt exists.

In acting on the motion of acquittal, the judge will view the prosecution's evidence in the most favorable light possible and determine if reasonable men could possibly conclude guilt beyond a reasonable doubt. If the state has clearly failed to meet its burden, the judge in most states may grant the motion and acquit the defendant. If the possibility of conviction exists he overrules the motion.

The Case for the Defense

The defense attorney presents his case following the same format as that of the prosecution. The defense will call witnesses and conduct direct examinations, followed by the prosecution's cross-examinations. However, the defendant is not required by law to present witnesses; he may waive the presentation of witnesses and submit the case based only on the state's evidence.

Even if the defendant presents witnesses, he is not personally required to testify. If he refuses to take the witness stand, the prosecutor or the judge is not permitted to call his lack of personal testimony to the attention of the jury. To do so will constitute reversible error. However, once the defendant takes the stand he is subject to the same cross-examination as other witnesses, including the disclosure of prior criminal convictions for the purpose of attacking his creditability.

Upon the completion of testimony of the final witness for the defense, the defense attorney announces that he rests his case.

Rebuttal and Surrebuttal

After the defense rests its case, the prosecutor is given the opportunity to call additional witnesses for the special purpose of refuting or rebutting the evidence presented by defense witnesses. Since it is for this sole purpose, the testimony received must be limited specifically to the nature and scope of the defense's case.

If the prosecution elects to call rebuttal witnesses, the defense may conduct a surrebuttal and present witnesses to disprove points raised or established during rebuttal.

Second Motion for Acquittal

After the receipt of all evidence, the defendant may again enter a motion for acquittal, challenging the sufficiency of the evidence and requesting the court to rule, as a matter of law, that the state has not met its burden of proof. In some jurisdictions this motion may be called a motion for a directed verdict. In jurisdictions permitting similar motions after the verdict, it is called a motion for judgment not withstanding the verdict. The criteria applied for the disposition of this motion are substantially the same as those used for disposing of the similar motion at the close of the prosecutor's case.

Instructions to the Jury

The judge is responsible for instructing the jury fully, clearly, and accurately on all issues which have been raised during the trial. The instructions traditionally include a definition of the crime with which the defendant is charged, the state's burden of proof, the presumption of the defendant's innocence, instructions relating to specific evidence in the case, and procedures for electing a foreman and returning a verdict.

During the progress of the trial, usually in chambers, the judge will give both counsel opportunity to submit suggested or requested instructions. In the absence of specific requests, he may utilize a "standard form" or "pattern instructions" generally applicable to all cases of a specific type. Or, if there are special circumstances in the case, he may require one of the counsel to draft a suggested instruction on the point in question.

Prior to the formal instruction of the jury, the judge prepares the set of instructions he plans to give the jury. Both counsel review them. If there is disagreement, there may be a conference between the judge and counsel. Subsequently, the judge prepares the final instructions, and counsel is given an opportunity to record any objections to them for possible appeal.

The judge instructs the jury in open court. He may read written instructions to them or orally instruct them from notes, depending on the requirements of his jurisdiction. Where written instructions are utilized, most jurisdictions either permit or require them to be taken to the jury room.

In many jurisdictions, the court must not only give proper instructions concerning the crime charged but also instructions relating to all lesser included offenses, which may be supported by the evidence in the case. For instance, in a prosecution for murder, if the evidence justifies it, the court should give instructions relating to manslaughter, and even possibly upon various degrees of assault. However, when there is no evidence to support a lesser crime, it is error to include it in the instructions.

Judge's Commentary on the Evidence

In some jurisdictions the judge, contemporaneously with giving the instruction, may summarize the evidence, analyze it generally, and emphasize what he considers to be the significant aspects of it. In this commentary, the judge must indicate that the jury may disregard his summary since the jury is the sole determiner of fact. While the judge, in those jurisdictions authorizing summarization and commentary on the evidence, has considerable latitude in his remarks, he cannot distort the evidence by becoming an advocate on one side's position, nor can he make remarks of a prejudicial nature. For instance, one case was reversed because a North Carolina judge referred to the defendants as "three black cats in a white buick."[4]

The judge is endowed with the privilege of commenting on the evidence so that he may utilize his experience and skill to aid the jury in reaching a just verdict. When he exercises the prerogative to comment he abandons his role as a "referee," and his assessment of the evidence may become a crucial influence because of the jurors' respect for his position. Whether granting the court the power to communicate its impressions of the evidence to a jury enhances the fairness of the trial depends not so much on a universal principle, but upon the competence, skill, and integrity of the individual judge. Even without the privilege of summarizing the evidence and commenting on it, the judge may exert tremendous influence on the jury by his general conduct, facial expressions, the inflections and deflection of his voice while ruling on objections, etc. (none of which is a part of the trial transcript which is reviewed on appeal).

Closing Arguments

After the instructions and the judge's summary or commentary have been given to the jury, the prosecutor and the defense attorneys address closing arguments to the jury. The primary purpose of the closing arguments is to give counsel an opportunity to summarize the evidence, comment upon it in relation to their theories of the case, and attempt to persuade the jury to accept their particular inferences and deductions.

Normally, the prosecuting attorney presents his argument first. The defense attorney then makes his presentation. Then the prosecuting attorney rebuts the defense argument. The attorneys are generally given liberal freedom in their range of discussion, the use of illustration, and the employment of persuasions, so long as they confine themselves to discussion of the evidence presented and normal deductions arising therefrom.

The defense attorney has wide latitude since, in an overwhelming majority of jurisdictions, the state may not appeal an acquittal. The only controls on his argument are his personal devotion to ethical standards and the contempt power of the court.

The prosecuting attorney is considerably more restricted since highly prejudicial remarks designed to arouse the passion of the jury or unjustified comments may result in reversal of the case. Following are some examples of remarks made by prosecutors which have resulted in reversals:

> "We all know the way of Jews' dealings in business and having their business dealings. These are God's chosen people, who the Bible says, shall gather into their arms all the wealth of the world."
>
> "Do you want to give this man less than first degree murder and the electric chair and have him get out and come back and kill somebody else, maybe you?"
>
> "A cold blooded killer."
>
> "This Black Murderer."
>
> "The time to stop a sexual fiend and maniac is in the beginning and not wait until after some poor little child or some little girl lost her life . . . or [is] mutilated."

Other reversed cases involved the prosecutor's reference to sensational crimes reported in the newspapers which had no relationship to the case, the inconsequential nature of a prison sentence because of the parole system, and imputation of dishonesty to the defense counsel.

Perhaps the restrictions placed upon the prosecutor's closing argument can best be summarized in the words of the United States Supreme Court, when it indicated that a prosecutor "may prosecute with earnestness and vigor—indeed, he should do so. But, while he may strike hard blows, he is not at liberty to strike foul ones."[5]

In the absence of a statute which provides the amount of time to be provided for closing arguments or the procedure whereby such time shall be determined, the judge may exercise discretion in establishing or limiting the time for final arguments. Normally counsel and the judge informally agree upon the amount of time to be consumed for this purpose.

Jury Deliberations

Following the closing arguments the jury retires to the juryroom for deliberations in an effort to arrive at a verdict.

Local statutes or court rules establish the appropriate procedures and conduct of jurors during deliberation. Common among these requirements is a restriction upon the jury communicating with anyone during its deliberation (except logistical matters with the bailiff or other officer responsible for their security and the judge in open court). A presumption of prejudice is created by unauthorized communications and must be dispelled before a verdict is acceptable. Many jurisdictions do not permit the jury to separate once deliberations begin. This restriction may require maintenance of the jury overnight in a hotel.

The length of time a jury may be required to continue its deliberations is generally considered a matter resting within the judge's discretion. When the jury has reported back to the court that it is unable to reach a verdict, the judge, after considering all the circumstances involved, may send it back to the juryroom for further deliberations and encourage it to reach a verdict. While the amount of encouragement the judge may give the jury to reach a verdict is presently the subject of considerable controversy, it is clear that he cannot be highly coercive by threatening to keep it for an extensive or indefinite period.

Under common law it was settled as early as 1376 that a unanimous verdict of the jury was required in criminal cases. This position was endorsed by the United States Supreme Court in 1898 and 1930. The jury trial provisions in the constitutions of most states either specify or have been interpreted to require a unanimous verdict. Some courts have gone even further and held that the unanimity requirements could not be waived by the defendant under any circumstances. However, the United States Supreme Court in two 1972 cases (*Johnson* v. *Louisiana* and *Apodaca* v. *Oregon*) upheld the constitutionality of less-than-unanimous verdicts. These cases leave the states free to provide for majority verdicts by constitutional provision, statute, or court rules. A number of states appear to be moving in that direction.

As an exception to the general rule, the constitutions in some states permit less than a unanimous verdict in misdemeanor cases. In Oregon and Louisiana, constitutional provisions permit less than unanimous verdict in felony trials, except in capital cases.

When the jury has arrived at a verdict or finds itself hopelessly deadlocked, it returns to the courtroom. If a verdict has been obtained it is received and announced. If a verdict has not been obtained and all reasonable methods of obtaining it have been exhausted ("hung jury"), the judge dismisses the jury and declares a mistrial.

After the jury has returned a verdict, counsel may request that the jurors be polled. The judge or the clerk then asks each juror individually if the verdict announced is his individual verdict. This process is designed to determine if each juror is acting freely according to his conscience or is the subject of group domination by his fellow jurors. If the poll discloses it is not a unanimous verdict (where one is required), the jury may be directed to return for further deliberations or dismissed and a mistrial declared.

If the verdict is "not guilty" the defendant is discharged and the case permanently terminated except in two states; Connecticut and Wisconsin permit the state to appeal a "not guilty" verdict. If the verdict is "guilty," the judge will set a sentencing date and remand the defendant to jail or permit his release on bail. If a "mistrial" is declared, the parties are in the same position as if no trial occurred, and the proceedings may be reinstated against the defendant.

In some jurisdictions, the jury may assess the amount of punishment. Depending on local procedure and the nature of the case, the jury may determine the sentence during their initial deliberations, or there may be a "two-stage" process wherein the jury determines its verdict, returns to the courtroom to hear additional evidence relating to punishment, and then returns to the juryroom to determine the punishment to be assessed. If the jury is unable to agree upon the sentence it becomes the responsibility of the judge to make the determination.

Motion for a New Trial

After the receipt of a guilty verdict, in most jurisdictions, the accused may file a motion for a new trial with the judge of the trial court within a period specified by statute (usually ten to thirty days). The motion requests that the judge set aside the verdict of the jury and grant a new trial because during the course of the trial the defendant had been deprived of a substantive right or the conduct or circumstances of the trial resulted in a prejudicial verdict.

Usually the grounds for a new trial are established by statute and may include such considerations as (1) the trial was held in the defendant's absence; (2) the jury received (and probably considered) evidence other than that properly presented in court; (3) the jury was guilty of misconduct (a juror was intoxicated, a juror communicated with a third party, etc.); (4) the court erred in a decision on a question of law during the trial (admission of tainted evidence, overruling a proper objection, etc.); or (5) the court gave an improper instruction to the jury.

In most jurisdictions, before an alleged error may be asserted as grounds for a new trial, the defendant must have objected to it at the time it was committed. However, when the error is of a fundamental nature, grossly affecting the accused's rights, it may be asserted at any time. A new trial should be granted for any error that significantly deprives the defendant of a fair trial even if that specific error is not enumerated in the statute authorizing the granting of a new trial. This is justified on the grounds of the judge's innate responsibility to assure fairness and impartiality.

Before a new trial will be granted, the defendant must establish that the error caused (or had the potential for causing) substantial prejudice, especially in cases where evidence of the defendant's guilt is clear and convincing.

On occasion, a new trial may be granted because of newly discovered evidence of a substantive nature. Normally, in such cases it must be established to the court's satisfaction that the evidence could not have previously been discovered by the use of due diligence prior to trial and that its impact, if introduced at a new trial, would possibly be sufficient for a jury to reach a different result. Evidence which is merely cumulative of that already presented or simply elaborates or expands issues already established is normally considered insufficient for granting the motion.

The decision on a motion for a new trial rests in the sound discretion of the trial judge, and the burden of establishing its necessity clearly rests upon the defendant. In the absence of a clear abuse of this discretion, appellate courts tend to support the trial judge's ruling.

The general theory justifying the motion for a new trial before the judge who presided at the trial is that errors should be corrected at the lowest level possible. During the trial the judge has supervised the presentations of witnesses, the receipt of physical evidence, the conduct of counsel, the preparation of instructions, and all general activity relating to the trial. Throughout the trial, various and sundry objections have been made and he has ruled on them. By presenting the motion for a new trial to him, he is provided with an opportunity to reevaluate his previous decisions and, as the judicial official most closely involved in the case, to make the initial determination concerning the fairness of the trial.

A hearing is normally held on the motion in open court before the judge. Since the motion only raises points of law, no jury is involved. Usually the prosecutor, the defense counsel, and the defendant are present. If the motion is granted, it is as if no trial had been held. If the prosecutor chooses, he may reinstitute the case and retry the defendant with no problem of jeopardy. In most cases, the motion will be denied, but it should not be regarded as dilitory since it provides an opportunity for a low-level review of the case prior to resorting to the appellate courts. If prejudicial error is present, the judge may correct it without burdening the resources of the appellate courts and the defendant.

Other Posttrial Motions

Some jurisdictions permit the filing of a motion in arrest of judgment which asserts jurisdictional defects, failure of the indictment or information to charge an offense, double jeopardy, and similar defects which normally have been raised by pretrial motions. Since such defects, if proven, are considered fundamental, this motion gives the court a second opportunity to review them prior to an appeal.

Most jurisdictions also permit the filing of a motion for reduction of the sentence, normally within a time period established by statute or within the same term of court.

Sentencing

After a guilty verdict, the court sets a sentencing date, usually two to four weeks later, for pronouncing the formal sentence. At the appointed time, the prosecutor, the defense attorney, and the defendant are present in open court before the judge.

If the court is responsible for determining the extent of punishment, the judge may, upon the suggestion of prosecution or defense, hear evidence relating to mitigation or aggravation of punishment. The scope of this inquiry is normally within the discretion of the judge.

Unless there is good cause shown (such as the pending of a motion for a new trial, the present insanity of the defendant, etc.), the court pronounces the sentence.

Discussion Questions

1. What might be the consequences of requiring less than a unanimous verdict for conviction or acquittal in a felony case? Would these consequences reduce even further the number of cases going to trial? Is this desirable?
2. When a jury is unable to reach a verdict, the judge usually declares a mistrial, and the prosecutor may retry the defendant if he chooses. Does such a procedure place undue hardship on the defendant? This procedure does not technically violate the prohibition against double jeopardy, but does it violate the spirit of the provision?
3. In light of numerous movements to standardize sentencing practices, should juries be permitted to assess punishment in individual cases?
4. After a guilty verdict, the judge may hear evidence relating to mitigation or aggravation of punishment. Such evidence probably would have been inadmissible during the trial. What are the advantages and disadvantages of such a practice?

Chapter Sixteen

The Sentencing Decision

The final phase of the criminal justice process at the trial court level is the decision concerning the type, length, and conditions of the sentence and its formal imposition. This decision may prove to be the most difficult of the entire trial. In conducting the trial and ruling on such things as admissibility of evidence, the judge may rely upon years of legal precedent and guidelines. But in pronouncing judgment in one particular case against one individual defendant, the judge has no such assistance. The many variables which motivated the offender to commit the crime and the type of sentence which may be most beneficial in correcting his deviant behavior may defy precise definition and the application of formulas. Not only is the decision difficult but highly critical, for if it is too harsh it may result in an embittered convict and a waste of human resources and potential. If it is too lenient it may deprive the individual of needed treatment and result in a career of continued criminal behavior.

The Sentencing Alternatives

Congress and the state legislatures provide the basic structure for the sentencing decision. Such legislation specifies who will set the sentence, the range of permissible sentences, the various alternative sentences that may be imposed, and the formal procedures to be followed in imposing and executing sentences.

In capital cases, many states place the responsibility of determining the sentence with the jury. Some thirteen states provide that juries will assess the penalty in some or all noncapital offenses. Historically, jury establishment of sentences is rooted in hostility toward colonial judges appointed by the British Crown. While many sound rationales exist to justify the retention of juries in this role, the preponderance of opinion today is that the function should be reassigned to judges to prevent inequities created by juries' lack of expertise. In a majority of states the sentencing decision rests solely with the trial judge, subject only to the limitations of applicable statutes.

The sentencing alternatives available to the judge, depending upon the jurisdiction, may include the payment of a fine, forfeiture of public office, imprisonment which is conditionally suspended (probation), imprisonment, confinement in a nonpenal treatment facility, a combination of the foregoing, or death. Depending upon the nature of the case, the court may order the defendant to make restitution to the victim, or forfeit the property utilized in the commission of the crime. If the crime is one involving addiction to drugs or alcohol or one in which insanity or sexual psychopathy is involved, the court may order the defendant to be confined in a specific treatment facility.

Fines

The court may assess a sum of money as the penalty for the offense. Frequently, the court costs—the costs of serving subpoenas, witness' fees, jurors' fees, and similar administrative costs—are imposed in addition to the fine. Upon failure to pay the fine, the defendant is committed to jail. Usually, he receives a *per diem* credit for jail time toward the fine assessed. For instance, the credit may be five dollars a day. If the defendant received a fine and costs of one hundred dollars, he would be released from confinement after serving twenty days. The term of confinement in lieu of payment may not exceed the jail sentence that the court could have imposed under the statute. Where the statute or ordinance provides only for a fine and no jail sentence, an indigent defendant may not be jailed because of his incapacity to pay the fine.

Probation

Probation is a technique permitting the court either to suspend the imposition of the sentence or to impose the sentence and suspend its execution. This is a privilege the court may extend to selected offenders which permits them to avoid incarceration by conforming to prescribed conditions of good conduct during the probationary period.

Most state statutes grant the trial judge broad discretion in either granting or denying probation. Some states nominally restrict this power by not permitting probation to be granted in certain types of serious cases (e.g., murder, arson, armed robbery, sale of narcotics, etc.), or restricting its use to first offenders only.

Some of the criteria utilized in exercising this discretion are (1) the seriousness of the offense; (2) the youthfulness of the defendant; (3) the absence of a criminal record; (4) employment prospects; (5) the interest of the defendant's family and his general home environment; (6) the availability of private medical or psychiatric treatment and the defendant's desire to undertake it; (7) capacity and willingness to make restitution to the victim of the crime; (8) the attitude of the community toward the crime and the political environment; (9) the conduct of the victim, especially in cases of statutory rape, etc; (10) the need to reduce the volume of jury trials, and the recognition that more guilty pleas may be obtained through the liberal use of probation; (11) securing the services of informants; or (12) a combination of the above considerations.

In granting probation the judge may prescribe a number of conditions that the probationer must meet. If the probationer fails to comply with the conditions, his probation is subject to revocation, followed by imprisonment. These conditions may include (1) restitution to the victim; (2) payment of court costs; (3) not violating any law during the probationary period; (4) avoiding questionable associates and places; (5) attending specified schools or educational institutions; (6) regulating the consumption of intoxicating liquor; (7) obtaining medical or psychiatric treatment; and (8) similar restrictions.

During the probation period, the probationer is normally assigned to a probation officer who is responsible for his supervision and control. In theory, the probation officer gives the individual advice and counsel and generally assists him in numerous ways to become a stabilized citizen. The degree of supervision varies from jurisdiction to jurisdiction. A probationer in one locale may be required to report once each week for an interview or discussion with his probation officer, periodic visitations may be made to his home, and additional supervisory or consultation devices may be employed. In another locale, a probationer may do nothing more than mail a brief report to the court periodically without any personal contact. Depending upon the jurisdiction and the bureaucratic arrangement, the probation officer may function as a part of the judiciary under the courts' framework or be a member of a separate executive department.

The pragmatic economic advantages of probation are obvious. In the case of an incarcerated offender the state is obligated to shelter, feed, clothe, and provide recreational facilities, medical care, and treatment programs for the prisoner. In addition, the state through its welfare program may support the defendant's wife and children during his confinement. The individual on probation, however, has the responsibility of earning a livelihood to support himself and his family. In addition, in most cases, as a condition of probation, the individual is required to make restitution to the victim and defray the administrative court cost involved in the case. Statistically, the offender on probation costs the state only one-tenth as much as the offender in prison. As one writer concludes, probation can convert society's officer, periodic visitations may be made to his home, and additional

On a national basis, slightly more than half of the individuals sentenced to correctional treatment are placed on probation rather than being sent to prisons. Based on numerous studies, between 60 to 90 percent of probationers successfully complete their probationary period.

The power to revoke probation for a violation of its conditions rests with the trial court. Usually such action is initiated by the filing of an application or petition requesting revocation either by a probation officer or the prosecuting attorney. Normally, after the petition is filed the court holds a hearing of an informal nature where the nature of the violation is explored and the defendant, represented by counsel, may present his side of the issue. The judge then renders his decision, which may be either to continue the probation or to revoke it and order the probationer confined.

As in other stages of the criminal justice process, discretion plays a significant role in revocation hearings. Because of the broad nature of the conditions of probation, most, if not all, probationers violate the conditions at one time or another during their tenure. Probation officers and prosecutors have a tendency to take no formal revocation action unless the violation is significant, generally amounting to the commission of another crime. Even when these officers, in the exercise of their discretion, do decide to file a request for revocation with the court, the judge also maintains a high degree of discretion in relation to revocation. Even if the evidence of the violation is clear and convincing, he may still choose to continue the probation.

Incarceration

Once the judge has decided against probation in a case, his alternative is incarceration. Depending upon the law of the particular jurisdiction, he may have two other decisions to make: (1) the location of the incarceration—work camp, reformatory, or prison, and (2) the length of the sentence.

The penalty for a particular offense is established by statute. The statute will usually provide for a minimum sentence and a maximum sentence. For instance, burglary might be punishable by a prison sentence of from one to seven years.

Some states require that a "definite" sentence be given. In the burglary case the judge would be required to specify the exact number of years to be served; e.g., he might sentence the defendant to two years.

Some states provide for an "indeterminate" sentence; that is, a sentence which is not stated in a specific number of years, but one which indicates a minimum and maximum term. A number of different sentencing structures exists within the indeterminate category:

- In a few states, the judge has no discretion over the length of the sentence since he is required to impose the statutory minimum and the statutory maximum. This system permits the parole officials broad discretion in determining when the prisoner should be released.
- Other states require the judge to impose the statutory maximum, but permit him to determine minimum sentence. Thus, he may increase the statutory minimum for the individual offender.
- In some states, the judge must impose the statutory minimum but may determine the maximum term. This permits the judge an opportunity to be lenient toward the individual offender.
- In still other states, the judge is granted the discretion to determine both the minimum and maximum sentence within the range provided by statute.

Extension of Sentences

Most legislatures have provided mechanisms for more lengthy sentences in certain types of cases. For instance, when it is established that the defendant is a "habitual criminal"—a person who has been previously convicted of one or more offenses—the minimum and maximum terms of the sentence may be increased under provisions of the applicable statute.

When a defendant is convicted of more than one offense during the same term of court, or when the convicted defendant is presently serving a prison sentence, judges in most jurisdictions have the option of imposing either concurrent or consecutive sentences. When concurrent sentences are imposed, the term served by the defendant applies to both sentences at the same time. When sentences are consecutive, time served is not applicable to the second sentence until the first sentence has been served. The authority to use consecutive sentencing in some states has been restricted to specific types of cases. Consecutive sentencing is not often used, but some judges, as an alternative, may give comparatively longer concurrent sentences on each charge. The general effect of consecutive sentencing is to delay substantially parole eligibility.

The Sentencing Process

After the trial results in a conviction (or the defendant pleads guilty), the court usually sets a date for sentencing two to four weeks later. During this interim, the motion for a new trial and similar post-trial motions may be filed by the defendant and heard by the court. Also, during this time the court may direct a general inquiry into the defendant's background in order to obtain data that will aid in the sentencing decision.

In most states the judge, at his discretion, is authorized to assign a probation officer to conduct a presentencing investigation. A few states require that such an investigation be made. In conducting the investigation, the probation officer may interview the police, the defendant, witnesses, the defendant's family and friends, social agencies having previous contact with the defendant, and similar sources. In selected cases the defendant may be requested to undergo psychiatric examination or other testing.

A complete presentencing report would contain a description of the offense and the general circumstances surrounding it, the defendant's prior criminal record, his educational background and employment history, comments on his marital relationship, family, religious affiliations, and general interests and activities, and medical and psychiatric data, if available. The primary function of the report is to assist the judge in determining if probation should be utilized in the case. Where probation is found inappropriate, the report may be used to determine the type and duration of the prison sentence in those states where judges possess such responsibilities.

The report is prepared for the judge's use, and much of what it contains would be inadmissible during the trial of the case. Since the report is in the nature of a social history, a majority of states leave it to the judge's discretion as to whether its contents should be disclosed, even to the defendant and his attorney. At the other extreme, several states make the report a matter of public record or require its disclosure to the defendant upon his request.

Since in most states the presentencing investigation is not required by law, the judge has an opportunity to use it when he feels additional information is desirable before sentencing. Other methods are used by some judges to obtain a degree of insight and guidance for sentencing. In some jurisdictions, when a defendant pleads guilty a postplea hearing is held where the judge receives testimony concerning the nature of the crime and the defendant's background. A postplea hearing, in addition to providing an opportunity to secure information about the defendant, permits the judge to verify the accuracy of the plea. In other jurisdictions, the judge may hold a hearing in mitigation or aggravation of punishment and permit both defense and prosecution the opportunity to present evidence which has a bearing on the severity of the sentence.

Although the formal sentencing process may vary between jurisdictions, it usually takes the following form:

- The judge in open court calls the case and assures that the defendant, his attorney, and the prosecutor are present.
- The judge asks the defendant if he would like to make a statement. More than half the states recognize the common law right of allocation—the right of the defendant to make a statement to the court prior to imposition of sentence. The defendant's attorney may be permitted to speak for him.
- The judge, if he chooses, may comment upon the presentencing report.
- The defense attorney is asked for his recommendation.
- In some jurisdictions a representative of the police may be asked for a recommendation.
- The prosecuting attorney is permitted to make comments.
- The judge announces his decision and pronounces judgment.

Although technically required in only a few jurisdictions, it is considered important for any possible subsequent actions in the case that the entire sentencing procedure be formally recorded. Also, after pronouncing sentence, the judge generally elaborates his reasons for the particular sentence and states the specific facts he relied upon in reaching his decision.

If the judge pronounces a probationary sentence, the probationer is released, subject to compliance with the probation conditions. In some states, the judge has the prerogative of ordering the probationer to serve a minimal sentence in the county jail (thirty to ninety days) prior to this release.

If the judge imposes a prison sentence, the defendant is remanded to custody for transportation to prison or released on bail pending appeal.

Discussion Questions

1. When a judge orders a presentencing investigation which he plans to use in sentence determination, should the contents of the report be disclosed to the defendant and the defendant be permitted to reply to the report? What would be the advantages and disadvantages of such a procedure, especially in those jurisdictions where a presentencing investigation is not required by law?
2. Should matters which were not proper evidence in a criminal trial be considered during the sentencing process?
3. Should the sentencing responsibility be removed from the judicial process and assigned to correctional officials?
4. Are standardized sentencing practices between courts desirable? If so, how may they be obtained?

Chapter Seventeen

Appeals and Postconviction Reviews

A system of criminal appeals was practically unknown in the early years of the United States. Most of the appeals procedures in existence today did not begin to develop until the late nineteenth century. Since that time procedures for review of criminal convictions have evolved until the defendant, as a matter of right, may obtain a review of his case in virtually every jurisdiction.

In most states the appeal is filed directly with the supreme court of the state. However, some fifteen states have intermediate appeal courts with criminal jurisdictions, and two states have specialized courts of criminal appeal with exclusive jurisdiction not subject to state supreme court review. In states that have intermediate appellate courts, the defendant may appeal as a matter of right to the intermediate court and, upon receiving an adverse decision, may petition the state supreme court for review. This second state review is a matter of discretion with the supreme court, and the petition in many cases will be summarily denied.

The federal court system has three levels of courts. The case is originally tried in the District Court, appealed to one of eleven Courts of Appeal or, at its discretion, to the United States Supreme Court.

The Nature of an Appeal

The primary function of the defendant's appeal is to review alleged errors of law—defects in the trial process. Relitigation of the facts is not permitted on appeal, and the appellate court will normally consider only the trial record in determining what constitutes the facts of the case. On rare occasions, appellate courts will reverse a conviction upon a premise that the evidence was clearly insufficient. Normally, however, if the court finds that there is sufficient evidence in the trial record from which reasonable men could draw a fair inference of guilt, the factual determination and verdict of the jury will not be disturbed.

Appeals, then, are based on the written record. In some jurisdictions, the lower misdemeanor courts are not courts of record; that is, they do not record the trial. In some of these jurisdictions, an appeal from such courts is made to a court of general jurisdiction (felony trial court). It totally retries the case and makes it a matter of record. Such procedures are called *de nova* trials.

In order to raise procedural defects as grounds for reversal, the court normally requires that objections must have been raised at the time of the alleged defect and at subsequent opportunities, such as the motion for a new trial. The major rationale for this requirement is that a defendant should not profit by his silence when remedial action could have cured the defect if objections had been raised. However, when the error is of such an overwhelming fundamental nature as possibly to deprive the defendant of a fair trial, the appellate court may forego this general rule concerning timely objections.

Before the appellate court will reverse, it must find the error to have affected substantially the defendant's rights and to have had the potential of affecting the results of the trial. The court may find a procedural error was committed but conclude that, in the total context of the trial, it was harmless, and affirm the conviction.

The appellate system was designed upon the assumption that there would be only a limited number of criminal appeals. No automatic review procedure exists and the defendant who desires a review of his case must initiate an appeal. There are only two major exceptions to this position. Some states provide for an automatic appellate court review of cases where the death penalty has been assessed, and military judicial procedure is to review all general courts-martial involving the imposition of a sentence of one year or more. A recent study of criminal appeals in the District of Columbia tends to refute the assumption of limited appeals:

> . . . appeals filed in fiscal 1966 represented 93 percent of all defendants convicted by trial in the District Court in that year . . . the percentage of those appealing increased gradually from 20 percent in 1955 to 36 percent in 1960, and more than doubled between 1962 and 1965.

> The rapid increase in recent years is probably attributable in part to recent judicial decisions which have made appeals by indigent persons more widely possible.[1]

The Appeal Process

Although the defendant in most cases has an absolute right to appeal, he normally must substantially comply with the proper procedures for appeal established by statute or court rules. His failure to do so may result in the dismissal of the appeal.

The defendant is required to give the trial court notice of his intention to appeal, either orally in open court or by filing a written notice. This action must be completed within a specified time which varies considerably between jurisdictions. In some jurisdictions, the defendant is also required at this time to request that certain logistical matters be undertaken, such as notifying the court stenographer to prepare the trial transcript and the court clerk to compile the requisite records, asking that the court provide for bail and release pending the appeal, and similar "housekeeping" tasks. In other jurisdictions the notice of appeal alerts concerned parties, or the court directs the necessary preparation.

After the notice of appeal the defendant must file a petition with the appellate court specifying those errors and issues upon which the appeal is based. Appellate judges will normally consider only those matters which have been raised by the defendant's petition, without concerning themselves with collateral questions. However, if a seriously prejudicial defect ("plain error") is discovered during the review process, the judges may resolve the case on that error even though it was not made an issue by the defendant.

A transcript containing the pertinent court documents and relevant portions of the trial testimony or rulings will be submitted with the petition. Many jurisdictions permit or require the submission of the total trial transcript ("casemade") to the appellate court. There is a growing trend, however, to submit only that portion directly relating to the alleged errors (by agreement of the defense attorney, prosecutor, and trial judge) and using other devices to minimize preparation costs and reading time. Supporting data, in the form of a "brief," is also submitted. Although the brief may vary in form between jurisdictions, the following excerpt from the Rules (1.7 and 1.8) of the Oklahoma Court of Criminal Appeals illustrates the substance generally required:

> The brief . . . shall contain: . . . A concise abstract or statement of the case, presenting succinctly the questions involved and the manner in which they are raised. . . . A specification of errors relied upon, specifically and particularly setting forth each error asserted and intended to be urged. . . . When the error alleged relates to the admission or rejection of evidence, the specification shall quote the full substance of the evidence admitted or rejected, stating specifically the objection thereto. . . . When the error alleged relates to the instructions of the court, the specifications shall set out the part referred to in *totidem verbis,* whether it be instructions given, or instructions refused . . . a brief argument, exhibiting a clear statement of the point of law or fact to be discussed . . . and the authorities relied upon in support of each point raised. . . . The Court may at any time after a cause is submitted, request counsel . . . to file with the Court . . . additional authorities . . . upon any proposition involved in the cause.

If no brief is filed with the transcript, the court will examine the record only to determine if the information or indictment adequately stated an offense, if the trial court had jurisdiction, and if there was sufficient evidence to convict. In some cases, the court may simply dismiss the appeal.

A copy of the defendant's brief must be served on the official representing the state in the appellate court—in some jurisdictions, the prosecutor; in others, the state attorney general. The prosecutor or the attorney general may file an answering brief opposing the propositions presented by the defendant.

Depending on the nature of the case and the state law, the case may be submitted to members of the court for decision based upon the briefs, or the court may request that the attorneys involved present oral arguments to a formal session of the court. Such arguments are limited primarily to the discussion of the points of law involved and the response to questions asked by the judges. After oral arguments the case is submitted to the members of the court for disposition.

The decision of the court will be subsequently announced by a written opinion. The opinion may be lengthy, involved, and complex, filled with legalisms and extensive citation of authority; or it may be a simple memorandum disposition consisting of a few sentences. If a judge does not agree with the decision or the specific legal reasoning of his colleagues, he may write a concurring or dissenting opinion. Copies of these opinions are released to the parties in the case, the news media, and the local bar association for immediate dissemination to the legal profession, and are subsequently published in permanent form where they serve as precedent and authority in future cases of a similar nature.

In rendering its decision, the appellate court has a number of alternative courses of action available. It may affirm the lower court decision. It may reduce the sentence imposed and affirm with this modification. It may reverse the lower court's decision and remand the case for a new trial in conformance with the opinion. It may simply reverse the decision based upon insufficiency of the evidence or other cause and order the defendant's release without permitting a second trial.

After the opinion has been issued, the losing party may, within a relatively short period of time, file a petition for rehearing. The petition for rehearing alleges that an issue decisive in the case has been overlooked by the court or that the decision conflicts with an existing statute or a controlling court decision which the court has not considered in its opinion. The court will review the petition, and, if granted, will resubmit the cases for consideration. If the petition is denied, or not filed within a specified time period, the original decision stands. This normally exhausts the defendant's rights of appeal.

Restrictions on the Right to Appeal

Normally, before an appeal can be lodged, it is necessary that the defendant exhaust his available remedies in the trial court. Depending upon the jurisdiction, the procedure involved may be a motion for a new trial, a motion to set aside the verdict, a motion for arrest of judgment, or similar procedural device. This requirement gives the trial court the opportunity to review all allegations of error so they may be corrected at the lowest possible judicial level.

Some jurisdictions require that the trial court must have rendered a final judgment before the appellate court will review the case. Based upon this ground, some states do not permit individuals to appeal when they have been sentenced to probation—since the imposition or execution of the sentence has been suspended. Other states do not permit probationers to appeal since in having received the benefit of "clemency" from the trial court, a technical waiver of the right is presumed.

An appeal may be filed even though the defendant has served the sentence that was imposed upon him. Since the conviction has possible consequences on the defendant's future employment, reputation, and other collateral matters, the issue of guilt is not mooted by execution of the sentence.

Most states have severe limitations on the prosecutor's right to appeal, based upon the concept of double jeopardy or undue hardship on the defendant. Two states permit absolutely no appeal at all. Most states permit the prosecutor to appeal adverse rulings in the pretrial stages prior to the attachment of jeopardy. A few states permit the prosecutor an appeal from an adverse ruling on a motion to suppress the evidence when he alleges that he has inadequate evidence to proceed to trial as a result of the suppression order. Three states have procedures whereby the prosecutor may appeal the verdict of the jury—but in the other forty-seven states the jury's verdict is final and binding upon the prosecutor.

Postappeal Reviews

A decision by the state supreme court, or by the intermediate court with a denial of further review, will usually constitute a final disposition of the case. However, if the error alleged involves the defendant being deprived of a right guaranteed by the Constitution, the defendant may seek further review of the case by filing a petition for a *writ of certiorari* with the United States Supreme Court.

The petition for a *writ of certiorari* specifies the nature of the case, the errors alleged, and previous court dispositions of the case. The writ is granted at the discretion of the Supreme Court. The percentage of such petitions granted has never been high, averaging only approximately 3 percent. If the writ is granted the parties file briefs, participate in oral arguments, and the Court makes a disposition of the case.

If the *writ of certiorari* is not granted (or if it has not been applied for), the defendant may resort to a collateral attack upon the judgment. Although various postappeal remedies may be available in different states, the most universal method of collateral attack is by petition for a writ of habeas corpus.

The remedy of habeas corpus developed early in common law, subsequently became a vehicle of political abuse in the fifteenth and sixteenth centuries, and was reformed as a means of assuring individual rights by the English Habeas Corpus Act of 1679. The act was not specifically extended to all the American Colonies, but subsequent actions by the states consisted of virtual reestablishment of the act's provisions. Its availability was subsequently guaranteed by the Constitution, the first federal judiciary act, and the constitutions and statutes of the states.

Any person imprisoned or restrained of his liberty (or someone in his behalf) may petition for the writ. The purpose of the writ is to provide a means of testing the legality of the detention. In most jurisdictions it is technically considered a civil remedy and, as such, may extend to cases of a noncriminal nature; e.g., a dispute between divorced parents over which should properly have custody of a child, an alleged alien being denied entry into the country by an immigration official, an individual contesting his commitment to a mental hospital, or a draftee questioning the legality of his induction into the military service.

In criminal matters, the writ may be utilized in such pretrial circumstances as an individual being held after his arrest by an officer without being taken before a magistrate, an individual being detained without formal charges being filed, a magistrate refusing to set bail, or a bail being set that is believed to be excessive.

Direct appeal is viewed as the proper method for attacking errors and procedural defects that occurred during the trial process. Some states, consequently, restrict the writ of habeas corpus by providing that it cannot be used as a vehicle for issues which should have been raised on appeal. Where this position is strictly applied, the writ may be utilized only to establish the court's lack of jurisdiction to impose the sentence. This would occur when the indictment or information failed adequately to allege the commission of a crime, the court was not authorized by law to try the offense (e.g., an inferior court imposing a felony sentence), the statute under which the accused was prosecuted was previously declared unconstitutional, the sentence which was imposed is in excess of that authorized by statute, or similarly narrow technical grounds. Other states interpret the phrase "lack of jurisdiction" liberally. They hold that when the defendant has been deprived of a basic constitutional right the proceedings technically become a nullity, and the court lacks jurisdiction to sentence. In these latter jurisdictions, the writ of habeas corpus is available to correct any denial of basic rights of due process, even though the issue more properly should have been raised on appeal.

The petition for the writ normally indicates who is detained, who is holding the prisoner, where he is being held, the cause or pretense of the restraint, and the reason such restraint is considered illegal. The petition is signed under oath by the prisoner or someone acting in his behalf. Depending on the state, the petition may be filed in the trial court, the court of original jurisdiction in the county where the defendant is being held, or with an appellate court. While in most cases the petition is filed in the trial court or one with equivalent jurisdiction, some states require that the petition must be initially submitted to the appellate court.

In most jurisdictions the judge will grant the writ without delay, unless the petition or annexed material fail adequately to allege an illegal detention. Such allegations are normally liberally interpreted. When the writ is issued, the person detaining the prisoner—usually the warden of the state penitentiary or the sheriff who is custodian of the county jail—is ordered to bring the prisoner before the court on a specified day and establish the cause for his detention. The appropriate attorney for the state (local prosecutor or the attorney general) will normally be served notice that the writ has been issued.

When the prisoner is produced, the judge will conduct a hearing into the legality of the detention. He may receive testimony, review records of previous proceedings, and make all inquiries necessary to resolve the issue. Upon finding that the detention is illegal he may order the release of the prisoner. However, upon finding no defects the prisoner will be remanded to custody. In most jurisdictions, there is a strong presumption in favor of the regularity of the trial, and the prisoner has the burden of proving defects.

Since habeas corpus is a civil proceeding, either the defendant or the state may appeal the decision made at the hearing. In this manner, the appellate court has a second opportunity, in addition to the regular appeal, to review the case.

After the defendant has been denied habeas corpus (or similar postappeal relief) in the state courts, he may file for a writ of habeas corpus in the federal district court if the matter involves a sentence imposed in violation of the Constitution or laws of the United States. In addition to the allegation presented in his state court petition, he must allege that he exhausted all available state remedies and present the record of the state proceedings where the alleged federal violations were considered.

The use of federal habeas corpus by state prisoners has expanded greatly in the past few years. The primary reason is the restrictive and highly technical nature of the state postappeal relief procedures and the willingness of the federal courts to rectify this shortcoming.

Federal habeas corpus has been held to be available in cases of violation of constitutional rights involving:

- prejudicial pretrial publicity
- illegal search and seizure
- involuntary confession
- deprivation of right of counsel
- trial dominated by presence of "mob rule"
- the knowing use of perjured state testimony
- prosecution suppression of material evidence
- insufficient evidence to support the conviction
- proceedings fail to conform to due process standards of the Fourteenth Amendment.

Federal habeas corpus has also been extended beyond the traditional restriction that the prisoner must literally be detained. It is available to challenge the legality of a sentence when the defendant is on probation or has been paroled from prison.

The results of the hearing in the federal district court are appealable both by the defendant and the state to the federal Circuit Court of Appeals. The decision of the Circuit Court is reviewable by *writ of certiorari* at the discretion of the United States Supreme Court.

Some jurists view with alarm the intervention of the federal courts via habeas corpus into matters involving state prisoners. It would appear that the number of such writs issued will decrease as states liberalize their highly technical and restrictive postappeal procedures to permit a prisoner an opportunity to be heard on the merits of his claim. Mr. Justice Brennan, perhaps attempting to quiet those disturbed by federal intervention, stated:

> . . . few indeed is the number of state prisoners who eventually win their feedom by means of federal habeas corpus. Those few who are ultimately successful are persons whom society has grievously wronged and for whom belated liberation is little enough compensation. . . . If the States withhold effective remedy, the federal courts have the power and duty to provide it.[2]

Even after the defendant has exhausted the procedures previously described, he may file successive applications for habeas corpus relief. Where the grounds have been previously heard and determined, the issuance of the writ may be denied at the judge's discretion if in his opinion, the ends of justice would not be served by another hearing. On successive applications, judges are also given greater flexibility in disposing of the matter as being frivolous and an abuse of the remedy.

Executive Review

The governors of the states and the President of the United States, within their respective jurisdictions, possess the power to pardon an individual convicted of a crime, to commute his sentence to one less severe, or to grant a reprieve which orders a delay in the execution of a sentence.

Unless otherwise restricted by constitution or statute, these powers are vested exclusively in the chief executive and may be exercised at his discretion. The only major control device is the power to impeach the executive for a gross abuse of this discretion.

Some states have provisions requiring the submission of a request for executive clemency to a board or committee which reviews it (and in some cases holds public hearings) and makes recommendations to the governor. Some states have a "clemency board" which must recommend affirmatively before the governor may act.

A pardon relieves the defendant of the service of any further sentence and destroys the determination of guilt. Legally, it is as if no conviction had occurred. The defendant cannot be retried. When a pardon is granted, there is usually strong evidence that the defendant did not commit the crime.

The commutation, unlike the pardon, does not vitiate the defendant's guilt but only affects the severity of the punishment. It may be used to relieve the harshness of the sentence, for instance reducing a death sentence to a term of life imprisonment or it may be used to effect the release of a prisoner by commuting the sentence to the time already served without conditions as to future behavior.

The reprieve neither affects the defendant's guilt nor the amount of punishment. It is a delay or a stay of execution of a sentence. It is most often used in death penalty cases to give the prisoner additional time to file for judicial relief. The courts also have the authority to grant stays of execution of the sentence.

Conclusion

There have been many cases in which the appellate process and postappeal procedures have been utilized to postpone the execution of the trial court sentence for many years. There are also documented cases of innocent men being imprisoned for the lack of adequate legal remedies to permit reexamination of the case on its merits. Sound criminal procedure requires a balance between obtaining some high degree of finality in a sentence and the assurance that due process requirements are met and that innocent persons are not confined. Perhaps the correct balance may be obtained by developing more effective state procedures and more imaginative handling of postappeal matters by the judiciary.

Discussion Questions

1. Today, appeals are based upon the written record of the trial, usually recorded by a court stenographer and subsequently transcribed. Appellate decisions are thus made on the "cold record." Modern technology has provided facilities for a complete audio-visual record of the proceedings. If adopted, what impact might a videotaped record have upon the appellate processes?
2. Should the prosecution have the right to appeal from an adverse verdict?
3. Considering the elaborate appeals procedures in most jurisdictions, what is the significance of the writ of habeas corpus?

4. Should the executive have the discretionary, and somewhat arbitrary, power to intervene in criminal cases by granting pardons, commutations, and reprieves, after the defendant has been lawfully convicted and sentenced by the judiciary?
5. If the decisions of the lower courts in a jurisdiction are frequently reversed on appeal, what conclusion can be formulated concerning their operation?

Chapter Eighteen

Incarceration and Release

Incarceration

The imprisonment of a man may occur immediately after the court pronounces his sentence and he chooses not to appeal or is denied release on bail pending appeal. If he has been released on bail pending appeal, his imprisonment may be delayed until the appellate court rules against him. If he has been placed on probation, he may be ordered confined after he has violated the conditions of the probation.

Treatment

On receipt of an individual by the prison, a program for him should be individually developed that will lead to his release at the earliest possible time. Extensive information about his psychological, medical, and social background should be collected. Competent staff should develop a treatment and training program tailored to meet his needs and minimize his shortcomings. Such programs should take into consideration his needs for additional formal education, training to develop vocational skills, and therapy designed to alleviate psychological problems. In addition, his program planners should consider the inmate's requirements for recreational, social, and religious activities, and other personal requisites. In short, the utopian program should be designed, insofar as possible, to overcome the many variable difficulties that resulted in the individual engaging in criminal conduct. The ultimate goal of this program should be the release of an adjusted individual, who is equipped to cope with himself in a complex society without resorting to prohibited conduct.

Release and Supervision

Once imprisoned the inmate may achieve release by a court reversing his sentence; the chief executive issuing a pardon or commuting the sentence to the time already served; the chief executive granting a conditional pardon requiring the inmate to meet certain specified standards of conduct or be subjected to the pardon's revocation; parole; mandatory conditional release when the inmate has served his entire sentence less credit given for good behavior, subject to revocation until the total sentence expires; and absolute discharge when the inmate has served the total sentence imposed. While many offenders serve their entire sentence and are released without legal restraints, more than 60 percent of prison inmates are released under parole conditions.

Parole is a procedure which permits the inmate to be released conditionally from prison before the expiration of his sentence. In theory, the treatment staff of the prison evaluates the inmate's conduct, performance, and attitude and, upon determining that his potential for successfully reintegrating into the community is satisfactory, processes his release. The inmate is subjected to the guidance, supervision, and control of a parole officer (whose functions parallel the probation officer described in a previous chapter). So long as the parolee's conduct meets acceptable standards during the period of parole, he remains free. If his conduct does not meet these standards, his parole may be revoked and he may be required to serve the remainder of his sentence.

In practice, however, in many cases, parole may not be granted when the inmate's potentials for success are at their peak. Since the granting of a parole is a matter of clemency and grace—a privilege instead of a right—the legislature is empowered to establish procedures for its administration or restrictions on its use. In exercising this power, some legislatures have provided that individuals convicted of particularly "heinous" crimes (such as first degree murder, forcible rape, and armed robbery) are not eligible for parole. In states where a definite sentence is imposed, the inmate may be eligible for parole only after he has served a specified portion of the sentence, usually from one-third to one-half. When an individual has received a life sentence, he is eligible for parole after the service of a specified time period prescribed by statute, usually around ten years. When the inmate is sentenced in a state utilizing an indeterminate sentence structure with a minimum and maximum sentence, he may be eligible for parole after the service of the minimum sentence, less any credit he may receive for good behavior.

In addition to the diversity of court sentencing practices and the rigidity of statutory provisions requiring inmates to serve minimum periods, the treatment officer's attempt to release the inmate at the most beneficial time is hampered by the provision that the treatment officer may only recommend the release. The ultimate authority, in all fifty states, rests with executive parole boards, committees, or other official groups. These boards are normally composed of five to ten members. In thirty-nine states the board members are appointed by the governor, and in four states appointment is made by other state officials. In four jurisdictions the boards are composed of *ex officio* members who, by virtue of their election to another office, automatically acquire a membership on the board (e.g., governor, secretary of state, state treasurer, etc.). Such appointment procedures provide an opportunity for selection of board members based solely on political considerations. They often result in a complete turnover of board membership when a new administration or political party gains office. In addition, many of the board members serve on a part-time basis. These methods of operation do not lend themselves to acquiring highly qualified professionals to serve in these critical decision-making positions. In the few remaining jurisdictions, the board consists of career employees selected through civil service procedures and protected by tenure in office.

In some jurisdictions, before an inmate may obtain parole he must have employment guaranteed upon his release. Once the inmate has served the minimum required time he may petition the parole board for his release. The board is not required to parole the inmate, nor is it required to justify its actions. It may deny the request for any number of subjective reasons, such as poor attitude, inadequate adjustment, the prisoner's lack of insight into his personal problems, not taking advantage of educational or vocational opportunities made available to him, etc. Most parole boards do not use sophisticated or tested criteria in making a release or retention decision, and each board member applies his individual discretion in passing on the case.

Several state boards do not hold hearings to decide the issue of the inmate's release but make decisions based on various reports contained in the inmate's file. Other states hold hearings but do not permit the inmate to be represented by counsel. The decision of the board is not appealable to the courts because its actions are based upon the premise that they fall in the category of executive clemency. No other functionary in the criminal justice process possesses so much unreviewable discretion.

Commenting upon the decision-making process employed by most boards the President's Crime Commission concluded:

> In the main, releasing authorities must depend on others for information about persons being considered for release. . . .
> Far too typically, overworked institutional case workers must attempt to gather information on a prisoner from brief interviews with him, meager institutional records, and letters to community officials. This information is often fitted into a highly stereotyped format. Frequently, the sameness of reporting style and jargon makes it very difficult for board members to understand the individual aspects of a given case and assess them wisely. This can lead to decisions which are arbitrary and unfair.[1]

When parole is granted a number of conditions are normally imposed upon the parolee. These conditions may include periodic reporting to the parole officer, obtaining approval for a change of residence or employment, abstinence from alcoholic beverages and drugs, supporting his family, and not leaving the jurisdiction without permission. The conditions may regulate his association with persons with criminal records, prohibit him from obtaining loans or purchasing an automobile, and, if single, require him to obtain permission before he may marry. Additional special conditions may be imposed. For instance, if the parolee was convicted for forgery, a condition may be that he refrain from establishing or using a checking account. If he was convicted for child molestation, a condition may be that he refrain from living in a home where there are young children.

If the parolee violates one of the conditions of his parole or commits a new offense, he is subject to having his parole revoked. At best, procedures for revocation may be described as informal. About half the states grant hearings before the parole board. A limited number of these permit representation by counsel, if the parolee retains one. A few states have made provision for state-appointed counsel for indigent parolees. However, a large number of states do not require a hearing and the parole board may simply revoke based upon the recommendation of the parole officer, the prosecutor, or other official. Currently, legislative guidelines are rather vague and ambiguous concerning hearing requirements; only a few judicial cases have examined the area of the revocation hearing. However, given the current judicial trend, it is highly possible that, if the legislatures fail to pass statutory provisions and/or parole boards do not establish administrative rules providing some semblance of due process, the courts will impose judicial guidelines and requirements.

Estimates indicate that approximately 35 to 45 percent of all adult parolees are recommitted. Most recommitals are predicated on violation of parole conditions, with approximately one-third being convicted of an additional felony. Assuming that these estimates are correct, approximately 55 to 65 percent of the parolees successfully complete the parole period.

The Purposes of Incarceration

The purposes of incarcerating convicted criminals have long been the subject of debate. Based upon the classical theory of crime causation, a person commits a crime of his own free will—he weighs the rewards to be obtained against the possible penalties he might receive if apprehended. Under this pleasure-pain rationale, the wrongdoer is punished and society obtains its vengeance. A second purpose for punishment is the belief that it has deterrent value. Theoretically, the offender, after he has been punished, will refrain from similar conduct. In addition, others who might contemplate the commission of a crime may be dissuaded by the knowledge that offenders will be treated harshly. A third purpose of confinement is to place the convict in a position where he may no longer prey on society. Some criminals, because of the nature of their acts, their previous backgrounds, and their threatening future potentials, cannot be permitted to remain in the community. Punishment under these circumstances is concerned with mere custody and segregation. A fourth purpose of punishment is reformation. Under this concept the sentence is designed, insofar as possible, to provide treatment and supervision for the individual, in the hope of being able to prevent future criminal acts.

The concept that the sentence should reflect the needs for correcting the deviant behavior of the individual has been a relatively recent replacement for the position that "the punishment should fit the crime." Less than three hundred years ago thieves' hands were amputated, rapists were castrated, and perjurers had their tongues removed.[2] In Connecticut, burning at the stake was permissible until 1797; the cropping of ears, branding and selling into servitude was statutorily authorized as late as 1829; and the use of stocks was not abandoned until 1905. The Connecticut courts in 1963 commented on the fact that public whippings were utilized as penalties for crimes until 1948 in Great Britain and until 1957 in Canada. The courts indicated, therefore, that a statute authorizing whippings as a penal sanction was valid and did not constitute cruel and unusual punishment.[3] Corporal punishment (executed by a leather strap four inches wide and 3½ to

5½ feet in length applied to the buttock, sometimes bared) was formally authorized in the Arkansas prison system in 1962, but was subsequently declared invalid by a federal court in 1968.[4] In a 1969 case, a federal judge commented: "For the ordinary convict a sentence to the Arkansas Penitentiary today amounts to a banishment from civilized society to a dark and evil world completely alien to the free world, a world that is administered by criminals under unwritten rules and customs completely foreign to a free world culture."[5]

A Philadelphia Court of Common Pleas in 1970 (*Bryant* v. *Hendrick*) found that similar conditions, including overcrowding, filth, homosexual assaults, brutal guards, and the absence of any rehabilitating program existed at the city's Holmesberg Prison.[6] A 1970 federal census of city and county jails indicated that over 25 percent of them were over fifty years old; some five hundred jails were built in the 1800's; and six jails built in the 1700's were and are still in service. Additional findings indicated that 85 percent had no recreational or educational facilities, 50 percent had no medical care facilities, and 25 percent were not equipped for visitors.[7]

The President's Crime Commission in 1967 found:

> For a great many offenders . . . corrections does not correct. Indeed, experts are increasingly coming to feel that the conditions under which offenders are handled . . . are often a positive detriment to rehabilitation.
>
> Life in many institutions is at best barren and futile, at worst unspeakably brutal and degrading . . . the conditions in which they [the offenders] live are the poorest possible preparation for their successful reentry into society, and often merely reinforce in them a pattern of manipulation or destructiveness.[8]

While the administrators of criminal law have made vast strides towards implementing the concepts that sentences should be individualized and offenders should be treated rather than punished, the preceding paragraphs clearly indicate that sentencing alternatives are not always based upon what is best for the offender. In many cases vengeance, retribution and deterrence still play a major role. Perhaps the best evidence of this is the fact that the death penalty still exists in thirty-seven states.

Currently the subject of extensive debate, the death penalty has been virtually abandoned in practice in the last few years. In the period from 1930 to 1966, there were 3,857 individuals officially executed in the United States. The highest number were executed in 1935: 199. The decline in recent years is significant: 1960—56, 1961—42, 1962—47, 1963—21, 1964—15, 1965—7, and 1966—1. The last execution in the United States occurred on June 1, 1967, but hundreds of people are still confined in cells in death row in various prisons throughout the country.

The 1972 Supreme Court decisions in *Furman* v. *Georgia, Jackson* v. *Georgia,* and *Branch* v. *Texas* held that the death penalty in these cases was cruel and unusual punishment, but it is clear from the opinions that the Court did not hold the death penalty unconstitutional under all circumstances.

After signing into law the Omnibus Crime Control Act of 1970, President Richard M. Nixon expressed pleasure that emphasis is being placed upon improving correctional programs and facilities and commented: "Too frequently correctional systems in the United States breed crime instead of returning rehabilitated men to society."[9]

The degree of efficiency and effectiveness ultimately obtained by law enforcement, prosecution, and the courts is not the paramount consideration in the subject of criminal justice. The quality of criminal justice and the ability of society to deal realistically with its crime problem will be directly dependent upon the quality of its correctional procedures and other programs directed toward isolating and eliminating the root causes of crime.

Discussion Questions

1. Does severe punishment serve as an effective deterrent?
2. Based upon the theory of executive clemency, parole boards possess virtually unreviewable discretion, the exercise of which is usually based upon hearsay and secondary data. Given these conditions, should a prisoner be entitled to a formal parole hearing with representation by counsel?
3. When a parolee is accused of violating the conditions of his parole, should he be afforded a formal revocation hearing and representation by counsel?
4. What are the most effective methods of eliminating the gross conditions that exist in many correctional institutions?

Chapter Nineteen

Reconciling Efficiency and Legality: Criminal Justice and the Rule of Law

The land is full of bloody crimes and the city is full of violence.
—Ezekiel, circa 500 B.C.

. . . crime, especially its more violent forms and among the young, is increasing steadily and is threatening to bankrupt the nation.
—Abraham Lincoln, 1836

Public order is the first business of government. . . . crime—and the fear of crime—has become a public malady. . . . Our country's laws must be respected. Order must be maintained. . . .
—Lyndon Johnson, 1967

The existence of crime, the talk about crime, the report of crime, and the fear of crime have eroded the basic quality of life of many Americans.
—President's Commission on Law Enforcement and Administration of Justice, 1967

. . . shoot to kill any arsonist or anyone with a Molotov cocktail in his hand . . . and . . . shoot to maim or cripple anyone looting. . . .
—Richard Daley, 1968

Our country is in trouble from within. The preservation of this Republic and the perpetuation of our free society under the rule of law are today challenged and endangered. Our system of criminal justice and constituted authority is under persistent assault.
—John McClellan, 1970

> Some might call this the era of the bizarre, the eccentric, and the erratic. . . . it certainly is an era in which the system of law and law enforcement is being seriously challenged. . . . Indeed, it is an era when emotion overrides reason. —J. Edgar Hoover

History reveals that in periods of great domestic turbulence there erupts the tendency to restrict accepted constitutional rights. Today, in some circles, the screams for "law and order" have almost reached hysterical proportions. For the sake of "effectiveness" and "safety," there exists a destructive readiness to forsake those rights for which government was established; and in their stead to construct make-shift expedients which are concerned with eliminating the symptoms rather than the causes of crime and disorder.

The prevailing mood in this country indicates a common concern over crime, violence, and general disorder. At the federal level, Congress has revised wire-tapping procedures, attempted by statute to emasculate constitutionally based decisions of the Supreme Court, appropriated millions of dollars to assist local law enforcement agencies, established a preventive detention process, and initiated other crime-fighting techniques and methodologies.

Other repressively oriented steps are being taken. At the local level, legislatures are increasing penalties; judges are assessing heavier sentences; parole boards are reacting more cautiously to requests; and probationary sentences, even though decreasing, are also being revoked at a more rapid rate. Municipalities are digging into city coffers to employ more policemen, to expand jail facilities, and to provide more manpower, equipment, and resources to continue the battle against crime in the same manner it has been fought for the past century.

Beyond any question, the criminal justice system is in need of improvement. Unfortunately, to date, most attempts to improve the effectiveness of the system tend to concentrate on techniques, procedures, methods, and even exotic equipment—most of which violate principles and rights.

Experience has demonstrated that an increase in police officers, tougher laws, harsher sentences, and similar punitive measures do not automatically result in a decrease in crime. Most efforts have overlooked or ignored the old maxim that the proper place to start curbing crime is not in the electric chair, but in the high chair. To reduce crime effectively, much more emphasis must be placed on a preventive rather than a punitive approach. Improvement in the educational system, slum clearance, better housing, job training, vocational rehabilitation, youth centers, drug clinics, the recruitment of highly educated and trained personnel into the criminal justice system, and similar strategies would undoubtedly place an extremely heavy burden on the taxpayer. There is little doubt, however, that the dividends reaped in reduction of crime, wanton destruction, and wasted lives would far exceed the investment.

Until our society learns to deal more appropriately with the many causative factors of crime and is willing to pay for meaningful programs, enforcement of the criminal justice system will continue to be extremely difficult. However, an interim expedient of abandoning the rule of law and legality as bulwarks of the system and foresaking our constitutional heritage in favor of fewer restrictions on our criminal justice agencies potentially condemns future generations to tyranny. While the price of crime is a heavy burden to bear, the lack of freedom is more grossly unbearable.

The constitutional guarantees which protect the citizen from unreasonable search and seizure, illegal arrest and confinement, and coerced or improperly obtained confession, and those which affirmatively provide right to counsel, trial by jury, and other aspects of due process, may inhibit the efficiency of the criminal justice system. Given these restrictions, no law enforcement agency will maintain a perfect record of crime solution, no prosecutor will compile a totally intact conviction record, and no court will consistently convict every prisoner at bar. The American system of criminal justice deliberately sacrifices much efficiency and effectiveness to protect the individual. Historically and philosophically, it is committed to the preservation of individual rights and liberties. Those who won American independence did not exalt order at the cost of liberty and believed that the final end of the state was to make men free to develop their individual faculties.

Under our philosophy of the rule of law, the prime standard is *legality*. The first concern in evaluating the local criminal justice system must be the assurance that it operates within the framework of constitutional and legal restrictions placed upon it. It must provide the positive protections of due process to all who are touched by it and, insofar as humanly possible, it must provide just and equitable dispositions.

These considerations do not mean that the efficiency with which the system accomplishes its tasks should not be a legitimate subject of great concern. Even though the requirements of due process may sometimes check rapid and inexpensive dispositon of criminal cases, due process should not serve as a rationalization or justification of gross mismanagement, excessive expense, or relative chaos within the institutional system. The dual standards of legality and efficiency are not necessarily incompatible. By merging legality and efficiency, an effective system of criminal justice may evolve—one which provides the defendant with full benefits of due process together with minimal delay and expense.

The purpose of this book was to describe the basic processes of criminal justice as they exist today. There was no intent to evaluate its operation analytically. Faced with the alternative of substituting efficiency for legality, however, the author is compelled to present some illustrations of how the efficiency of the system may be increased while simultaneously preserving the rights of defendants. The following pages contain a number of evaluative criteria which may be applied to local criminal justice systems. They are not intended to be exhaustive but only indicate the possibility of a rational compromise between efficiency and legality.

Improving Police Efficiency

The techniques of sound police administration are not new or unique. Business and industry have utilized management methods for years in an effort to compete for the consumer's dollar and to produce their goods and services in the most efficient and effective manner possible. Those who failed to devote sufficient attention to sound management concepts either found their growth inhibited and eventually merged with successful firms, or ended their existence in the bankruptcy courts. Police departments are not faced with the pressure of producing a profit. No stockholders clamor for quarterly dividends. The police administrator knows that his governmentally financed organization will never go bankrupt. Nonetheless, unfortunately, a majority of our police departments today suffer from improper management of the resources that are made available to them. Sound administrative methods could increase the effectiveness of virtually any police department in the country, without diluting basic rights.

Lawful Arrest

One evaluator which can be applied is based primarily upon existing police records: *Was the suspect taken into custody for a specific criminal act as required by law?*

It has been a long-standing principle that an officer cannot arrest an individual unless he possesses a warrant, observes the offense, or in certain types of cases has reasonable and probable cause to believe that a crime has been committed. An individual cannot be legally arrested on such vague and nonexistant charges as suspicion, investigation, general principles, and similar nondescriptive reasons. Yet individuals are daily arrested and detained in this manner. Such activity in a community should immediately serve as a warning sign of abuse of police authority—and of inefficiency in police management.

Pretrial Detention

Assuming that the arrest was lawful, the question should be raised: *Was the physical arrest necessary?*

On detecting a violation, a police officer has a number of practical alternatives available to him. Utilizing his discretion, he may choose to ignore the violation, warn the violator, issue a citation requiring either payment of fine or appearance in court, refer the matter to some other official for investigation and disposition, or take the suspect into physical custody.

Beyond the fact that a physical arrest deprives the individual of his freedom, it is an expensive process. During his confinement the jurisdiction must provide physical facilities for housing, personnel to insure physical custody, food, medical services if needed, protection for his property such as an automobile or personal possessions, and personnel and equipment to transport him to various legal hearings. If the individual is unable to post bond or secure his release, this confinement and expense may continue for several months.

Those concerned with this problem should review the local law to determine if a broad application of citation issuance is permitted and, if not, advocate the necessary changes. The types of physical arrest made by police should be reviewed. The bond policies of the courts should be surveyed.

Where the defendant has a valid employment status, has strong family relationships in and ties to the community, has generally good reputation or character, has no serious prior criminal record, coupled with the general nature of the offense, or any combination of these factors, little ground can be found for pretrial detention. This is an area where democratic, humane principles can be applied and result in considerable savings in public funds.

Custodial Rights

Once the decision is made not to cite, but to effect physical custody, the critical concern becomes: *Are the defendant's custodial rights safeguarded?*

The police should warn every arrested person of his constitutional rights. He may remain silent; statements given by him to police or others may be used against him in court; he has a right to have counsel with him during any interrogation; and, if he is indigent and desires counsel, a court must appoint counsel before the interrogation proceeds.

Every arrested person should be taken before a judicial officer without unreasonable delay. The appearance before the judicial officer should occur in a quiet dignified manner and in physical surroundings appropriate to the administration of justice. The case should receive personal, individual treatment. The proceedings should be conducted in such a way as to assure that the defendant is effectively informed of his rights and the action that is being taken against him.

The police should not view the custody of the accused simply as an expedient to the investigation. A few years ago, a very prevalent practice was that an individual suspected of committing a crime was arrested on a minor charge and detained pending investigation. He was not allowed counsel or other assistance and might be held several hours while officers completed a portion of their investigation or subjected him to extensive interrogation. The courts have rebelled against this practice, and in most cases evidence obtained utilizing these means will be viewed as tainted and excluded from use in the case.

Of course, it is extremely difficult, if not impossible, to evaluate and determine if every defendant receives his custodial rights. However, there are a number of check points which may be indicative of what practices exist locally.

> Are defendants booked on specific charges or are vague charges like "vagrancy" or "loitering" used extensively within the department?
>
> Are a large number of defendants released by police without processing them through the prosecutor's office or the court?
>
> What is the average time between booking and appearance before a judicial officer?
>
> Are judges available at odd hours to handle initial appearance?
>
> Do *written* policy statements or procedures exist within the police department concerning the processing of defendants and affording them their rights?
>
> How much formal training do police officers receive in the areas of criminal procedure? Do prosecutors and judges participate in the training program? (If officers are untrained in criminal procedure, it is doubtful they can properly process a defendant.)

Right to Counsel

Very few laymen have a working knowledge of the law. Charged with a crime, even an intelligent and well-educated individual would generally be incapable of determining whether the formal accusation were technically valid. He probably would be unfamiliar with the relatively complex rules of evidence. Without counsel at his side, he might well be tried on a defective accusation and convicted upon incompetent, irrelevant, or inadmissible evidence.

In 1963, the United States Supreme Court, recognizing this problem, held that where the defendant was indigent and unable to retain counsel, the state must provide him with counsel in all felony cases and in 1972 went beyond this position and decreed that this right should be expanded to all criminal cases, both felony and misdemeanor.

Responses to this decision have varied. Some trial courts have appointed counsel on an *ad hoc* day-to-day improvisational basis. Some have responded with a public defender system, an office headed by a public official and supported by state funds. Others have used a private defender system, with the office organized as a corporation and supported by private funds. Some have used a public-private defender system, which is supported by both sources of funds.

Regardless of the means of providing counsel, it should be in accordance with a *systematic* and *widely publicized* plan. The conclusions of numerous authorities on the subject are that the worst inequities occur when there is no organized or systematic approach to the problem at the local level. Some evaluators can be applied locally.

Does a systematic plan exist which provides a means for appointment of counsel?

Is the plan well publicized?

Is the local bar association involved in the plan or do they endorse it?

Does the plan guarantee the integrity of the relationship of lawyer and client?

Are the plan and the lawyers serving it free from adverse political influence and subject only to judicial supervision?

Does the plan also provide for investigatory, expert, and other services necessary for an adequate defense?

Does the defender have a convenient and dignified office with a sufficient legal library?

Prosecution

For practical purposes the local prosecutor has virtually unlimited power to initiate or refuse the prosecution of a case. The prosecutor, director of the state's case, utilizing the vast discretion he possesses, holds the power to decide the fate of the case at an extremely early stage. Commenting on the role of the prosecutor, the President's Commission on Law Enforcement and the Administration of Justice said:

> The key administrative officer in the processing of cases is the prosecutor. Theoretically, the examination of the evidence against a defendant by a judge at a preliminary hearing, and its reexamination by a grand jury, are important parts of the process. Practically, they seldom are because a prosecutor seldom has any difficulty in making a prima facie case against a defendant. In fact most defendants waive their rights to preliminary hearings, and, much more often than not, grand juries indict precisely as prosecutors ask them to do. The prosecutor wields almost unlimited sway over the pretrial progress of most cases. He decides whether to press a charge or drop it. He determines the specific charge against a defendant. When the charge is reduced, as it is in as many as two-thirds of all cases in some cities, the prosecutor is usually the official who reduces it.

It is extremely difficult for one not trained in criminal procedure and the operation of the court system to evaluate the office of the prosecutor. This difficulty is partially due to lack of technical knowledge and, partially to the compound prosecutorial role within the system. Ethically and legally, the prosecutor's function is not necessarily to convict but "to see that justice is done." Theoretically, he must be concerned with representing the state, while at the same time assuring that the defendant's rights are protected. Through the use of his discretion, he is expected to make decisions based not only upon the statutory law, but also upon the individual characteristics of the accused, the facts of the case, and other extenuating circumstances.

However, there are some universal evaluators that can be applied to eliminate obstacles to effective prosecution and to test the general operation of the office.

> Is the prosecutor's position a full-time job or is he permitted to maintain a private practice as well?
>
> Is the salary adequate to encourage qualified individuals to run for the office? Is it adequate to retain them as career prosecutors?
>
> Is there an adequate number of assistant prosecutors to handle the volume of work load?
>
> Is there adequate clerical personnel?
>
> Is his law library adequate?
>
> Are the prosecutor and his staff provided with funds to attend professional meetings and schools?

Does the prosecutor instruct in the local police training program?

What is the working relationship between the prosecutor's office and the police?

What is the volume of police cases that the prosecutor refuses to prosecute? Why was prosecution refused? (The answer to these questions may reflect adversely either upon the police or the prosecutor, depending upon the circumstances.)

In what percentage of cases does he reduce the charges? Why?

The last three questions are designed for the purpose of problem discovery. The answers to these questions will have to be interpreted in light of all surrounding circumstances.

Delay in the System

One of the greatest criticisms of the system is the lengthy delay between the time the defendant is arrested and the disposition of the case, which in some cases may exceed two years. This situation causes many deleterious effects. It encourages dismissals, coerces pleas of guilty, gives defendants an opportunity to manipulate the system, decreases respect for the system on the part of offenders, and adversely affects public confidence.

As a standard, the President's Commission recommended a model time table which would provide for trial within twelve weeks. Although this must be regarded as the model or ultimate system, it does provide a standard against which local systems can be measured.

The causes of delay within the court system are basically inefficient management, lack of resources, dilatory actions by defense counsel, and increasing volume of cases. Some areas of investigation for evaluation of delay are:

Do judges regularly hold court several days each week?

Does the court function only part of the day?

If more than one judge is present within the community, is there a system of shifting overload cases to another court which has a less congested docket?

Are judicial vacancies filled immediately?

Are judicial vacations reasonable? (Some vacations may be as long as four months.)

Are sound internal management principles being applied? Are docket entries still handwritten? Are forms in need of redesign? Are filing systems burdensome and inadequate?

> Is adequate personnel available to perform ministerial functions? Is the judge still responsible for ordering supplies, supervising personnel, keeping facilities and equipment functional, and similar custodial tasks?
>
> Are the business affairs of the court handled by a professional aide who continuously gathers and assesses information for scheduling, establishing calendars and dockets, and otherwise expediting the work of the court?

The mechanical operation of the court system lends itself to the same principles of management that are applied in business. Many courts, however, have continued operations without adapting to modern management techniques.

There will be some situations that the applications of the skills of an efficiency expert will not correct. Where obstacles to the speedy trial are created because of organizational problems in the system or inadequate authorized personnel, the obvious remedy is to seek court reorganization and authorization of additional personnel through the legislative process.

Conclusion

The criminal justice system is organizationally complex. Added to this complexity are the individual personalities of its officials, the vast amount of discretion that each possesses, the traditions and customs of each community, the local political climate, general public attitudes, and hundreds of other variables. It can easily be recognized that the evaluation and improvement of such a system is a tremendous task.

No system is better than the men that collectively compose it. Perhaps the greatest improvements in criminal justice efficiency will not come from a concerted effort to adopt sound management techniques in police departments, the establishment of a career program in the prosecuting attorney's office, the computerization of court records, or similar strategies. Perhaps the greatest efficiency will occur when imaginative, dedicated, and educated individuals are recruited into the system. If these individuals have the courage to challenge archaic ideas, to initiate new programs with socially based goals, and to control their efforts firmly within the concepts of the rule of law, then legality will not only function with efficiency, but they will coexist as the twin standards of the system.

But while we impatiently wait for the system to adopt internally sound operational principles and recruit into its ranks the imaginative innovator, we cannot permit ourselves to succumb to the repressive, quick solutions which involve forfeiting precious rights and values. To subscribe to more efficiency, at the cost of individual liberty, is to crucify the rule of law on a cross of hysteria.

Discussion Questions

1. What is "justice"? What criteria can be used to determine what is just and unjust?
2. What is the distinction between due process and justice?
3. Some procedures, such as releasing a defendant on his own recognizance, serve both to preserve the defendant's rights and dignity and to create a more efficient, less expensive criminal justice system. Why then are they not implemented in some jurisdictions?
4. What should be the goal of the criminal justice system?

NOTES

Chapter 1

[1] Jerome Frank, *Law and the Modern Mind,* 6th ed. (New York: Coward-McCann, 1949), p. vi.

Chapter 2

[1] President's Commission on Law Enforcement and Administration of Justice, *Task Force Report: Drunkenness* (Washington, D.C.: Government Printing Office, 1967), p. 1.

[2] Ibid., pp. 2-4.

[3] Ibid., pp. 3-4.

[4] Norval Morris and Gordon Hawkins, *The Honest Politician's Guide to Crime Control* (Chicago: University of Chicago Press, 1970), p. 6.

[5] Charles E. O'Hara, *Fundamentals of Criminal Investigation,* 2nd ed. (Springfield, Illinois: Charles C. Thomas Publishers, 1970), p. 544. Some authorities estimate the number of illegal abortions performed nationally exceeds two million annually. Cf. David Reuben, *Everything You Always Wanted to Know about Sex but Were Afraid to Ask* (New York: Bantam Books, 1969), pp. 310-311.

[6] United Press International, "34,175 Abortions Reported," (Lansing, Michigan: *State Journal,* January 7, 1971), p. A-19. The estimated ratio of abortion to births for residents of the state only was 198 abortions per every 1,000 live birth, based on State Health Department data.

[7] Alfred Charles Kinsey, Wardell B. Pomeroy and Clyde E. Martin, *Sexual Behavior in the Human Male* (Philadelphia: W. B. Saunders Co., 1948), p. 392.

[8] Arthur Everett, Associated Press, "Noble Experiment Inaugurated 50 Years Ago" (Lansing, Michigan: *The State Journal,* October 28, 1969), p. A-1.

[9] Ibid.

[10] Thomas C. Schelling, "Economic Analysis and Organized Crime," in *Task Force Report: Organized Crime* (Washington, D.C.: Government Printing Office, 1967), pp. 123, 124, 125.

[11] Ibid., p. 125.

[12] Ibid., p. 124.

[13] President's Commission, *Task Force Report: The Courts,* p. 107.

Chapter 3

[1] *Illinois Revised Statutes,* Chapter 125, Sections 14, 15, 17, 18, 30, 31 and 82.

Chapter 4

[1] 180 F. Supp. 71 (S.D., N.Y., 1960).

[2] Livingston Hall, Yale Kamisar, Wayne LaFave and Jerold Isarel, *Modern Criminal Procedure,* 3rd ed. (St. Paul: West Publishing Company, 1969), p. 8.

[3] John Edgar Hoover, *Crime In The United States* (Washington, D.C.: Government Printing Office). This report is issued annually as a part of the Uniform Crime Reports program and contains a compilation of crimes reported to the police agencies of the country.

[4] J. Shane Creamer, *The Law of Arrest, Search and Seizure* (Philadelphia: W. B. Sanders Co., 1968), p. 53.

[5] Rollins M. Perkins, *Criminal Law and Procedure,* 3rd ed. (Brooklyn: The Foundation Press, 1966), p. 792.

[6] *Dilger* v. *Commonwealth,* 88 Ky 550, 11 S.W. 651 (1889).

[7] Perkins, *Criminal Law and Procedure,* pp. 791-802.

[8] Ibid.

[9] *Michigan Statutes Annotated,* Section 28.87; *Michigan Compiled Laws 1948,* Section 764.15.

[10] *People* v. *Ross,* 60 Calif. Rptr. 254, 429 P. 2d 606 (1967).

[11] *Bringer* v. *United States,* 338 U.S. 160, 69 Sup. Ct. 1302, 93 L. Ed. 1879 (1949).

12 *Beck* v. *Ohio,* 379 U.S. 89, 85 S. Ct. 223; 13 L. Ed. 2d 142 (1964). Cf. *Draper* v. *U.S.,* 358 U.S. 307, 79, S. Ct. 329, 3 L. Ed. 2d 327 (1959); *Jones* v. *U.S.,* 362 U.S. 257, 80 S. Ct 725, 4 L. Ed. 2d 697 (1960); *Rugendorf* v. *U.S.,* 376 U.S. 528, 84 S. Ct. 825 (1964); *Aguilar* v. *Texas,* 378 U.S. 108, 84 S. Ct. 1509, 12 L. Ed. 2d 723 (1964); *U.S.* v. *Ventresca,* 380 U.S. 102, 85 S. Ct. 741, 13 L. Ed. 2d 684 (1965).

13 Creamer, *Law of Arrest,* p. 53.

14 *Giordenello* v. *United States,* 357 U.S. 480, 78 S. Ct. 1245, 2 L. Ed. 2d 1503 (1958).

15 Dissenting opinion in *Jones* v. *United States,* 362 U.S. 257, 80 S. Ct. 725, 4 L. Ed. 2d 697 (1960).

16 *Malone* v. *Carey,* 17 Cal. App. 2d 505, 62 P. 2d 166 (1936).

17 *Commonwealth* v. *Crotty and Others,* 92 Mass. 403 (1865).

Chapter 5

1 President's Commission on Law Enforcement, *Challenge of Crime in a Free Society,* p. 10.

2 Wayne R. LaFave, *Arrest: The Decision to Take a Suspect into Custody* (Boston: Little, Brown and Co., 1965), pp. 83-143.

3 Ibid., pp. 144-152.

4 Ibid., pp. 437-482.

5 F. K. Heusseustamm, "Bumper Stickers and the Cops," *Transaction,* 8 (February, 1971), p. 32.

6 Herman Goldstein, "Police Discretion: The Ideal Versus the Real," in Arthur Niederhoffer and Abraham Blumberg *The Ambivalent Force: Prospectives on The Police* (Waltham, Massachusetts: Ginn and Company, 1970), p. 149; and Herman Goldstein, "Full Enforcement vs. Police Discretion Not to Invoke the Criminal Process," in A. F. Brandstatter and L. A. Radelet, eds. *Police and Community Relations:* A Sourcebook (Beverly Hills: Glencoe Press, 1968), pp. 381-391.

7 President's Commission on Law Enforcement, *Task Force Report: The Police,* p. 19.

Chapter 6

1 Michigan State University, *A National Survey of Police and Community Relations* (Field Surveys, Report Submitted to President's Commission on Law Enforcement and Administration of Justice) (Washington, D.C.: Government Printing Office, 1967), pp. 327-336.

2 President's Commission on Law Enforcement, *Task Force Report: The Police,* pp. 183, 184.

[3] 392 U.S. 1, 88 S. Ct. 1868, 20 L. Ed. 2d 889 (1968).

[4] *Sibron* v. *New York, Peters* v. *New York,* 392 U.S. 40, 80 S. Ct. 1889, 20 L. Ed. 2d 917 (1968).

[5] President's Commission on Law Enforcement, *Task Force Report: The Police,* pp. 183-184.

Chapter 7

[1] 232 U.S. 383, 34 S. Ct. 341, 58 L. Ed. 652.

[2] 338 U.S. 25, 69 S. Ct. 1359, 93 L. Ed. 1782.

[3] 367 U.S. 643, 81 S. Ct. 1684, 6 L. Ed. 2nd 1081.

[4] For example, see *Irvine* v. *California,* 347 U.S. 128, 74 S. Ct. 381, 98 L. Ed. 561 (1954). Also see Justice Murphy's dissenting opinion in *Weeks* v. *United States,* and Hall et al. *Modern Criminal Procedure,* pp. 217-220.

[5] *Ker* v. *California,* 374 U.S. 23, 83 S. Ct. 1623, 10 L. Ed. 2d 726 (1963).

[6] *United States* v. *Rabinowitz,* 339 U.S. 56, 70 S. Ct. 430, 94 L. Ed. 653 (1950).

[7] *Stanford* v. *Texas,* 379 U.S. 476, 85 S. Ct. 506, 13 L. Ed. 2d 431 (1965). Justice Stewart's opinion in this case provides an excellent historical review and rationale for this requirement.

[8] *Harris* v. *United States,* 331 U.S. 145, 67 S. Ct. 1098, 91 L. Ed. 1399.

[9] 395 U.S. 752, 89 S. Ct. 2034, L. Ed. 2d.

[10] 391 U.S. 543, 88 S. Ct. 1788, 20 L. Ed. 2d 797 (1968).

[11] *Chapman* v. *United States,* 365 U.S. 610, 81 S. Ct. 776, 5 L. Ed. 2d 828 (1961).

[12] *Stoner* v. *California,* 376 U.S. 483, 84 S. Ct. 889, 11 L. Ed. 2d 856 (1964).

[13] *Higgins* v. *United States,* 209 F. 2d 819 (D.C. Cir., 1954).

[14] *Johnson* v. *Zerbst,* 304 U.S. 458, 58 S. Ct. 1019, 82 L. Ed. 1461 (1938).

[15] *Carroll* v. *United States,* 267 U.S. 132, 45 S. Ct. 280, 69 L. Ed. 543 (1925); *Husty* v. *United States,* 282 U.S. 694, 51, 5 Cf. 240, 75 L. Ed. 629 (1931); *Brinegar* v. *United States,* 338 U.S. 160, 695 Cf. 1302, 93 L. Ed. 1879 (1949); and *Chambers* v. *Maroney, op. cit.* (1970).

[16] *Camara* v. *Municipal Court,* 387 U.S. 523, 87 S. Ct. 1727, 18 L. Ed. 2d 930 (1967).

[17] *See* v. *City of Seattle,* 387 U.S. 541, 87 S. Ct. 1737, 18 L. Ed. 2d 943 (1967).

[18] *Harris* v. *United States,* 390 U.S. 234, 88 S. Ct. 992, 19 L. Ed. 2d 1067.

[19] 362 U.S. 217, 80 S. Ct. 683, 4 L. Ed. 2d 688 (1960).

Chapter 8

[1] Fred Inbau and John Reid, *Criminal Interrogation and Confessions* (Baltimore: The Williams and Wilkins Company, 1962), p. 1, 204; and Charles E. O'Hara,

Fundamentals of Criminal Investigation, 2nd ed. (Springfield, Illinois: Charles C. Thomas Publisher, 1970), p. 85.

2 Yale Kamisar, "Equal Justice in the Gatehouses and Mansions of American Criminal Procedure," in Yale Kamisar et al., *Criminal Justice in Our Time* (Charlottesville: Rector and Visitors of the University of Virginia, 1965); and A. Kenneth Pye, "The Supreme Court and The Police: Fact & Fiction," 57 *Journal of Criminal Law, Criminology and Police Science,* 404 (1966).

3 367 U.S. 568, 81 S. Ct. 1860, 6 L. Ed. 1037 (1961).

4 For the "subtler devices" Justice Frankfurter *may* have reference to, see Fred Inbau and John Reid, *Criminal Interrogation and Confessions,* and Richard Arther and Rudolph Caputo, *Interrogation for Investigators* (New York: William C. Copp and Associates, 1959).

5 318 U.S. 332, 63 S. Ct. 608, 87 L. Ed. 819.

6 354 U.S. 449, 77 S. Ct. 1356, 1 L. Ed. 2d 1479.

7 *The Omnibus Crime Control and Safe Street Act of 1968* attempts to repeal the *McNabb-Mallory* rule. Because the Act also involves the attempted repeal of other pertinent Supreme Court decisions, an examination of it is reserved for a subsequent portion of this chapter.

8 297 U.S. 278, 56 S. Ct. 461, 80 L. Ed. 682.

9 378 U.S. 1, 84 S. Ct. 1489, 12 L. Ed. 2d 653.

10 378 U.S. 478, 84 S. Ct. 1758, 12 L. Ed. 977.

11 384 U.S. 436, 86 S. Ct. 1602, 16 L. Ed. 2d 694 (1966). The Constitutional basis for the decision was the Sixth Amendment to the Constitution which guarantees an individual "assistance of counsel for his defense." *Gideon* v. *Wainwright* (to be examined in a subsequent chapter) held in 1963 that the Fourteenth Amendment "due process" made Sixth Amendment right to counsel obligatory on the states.

12 91 S. Ct. 643.

13 Sidney E. Zion, "Advice to Suspect Found Police Aid," *New York Times,* February 28, 1966, p. 18C and "Criminal Justice: Concern About Confessions," *Time Magazine,* April 29, 1966, p. 65.

14 Seeburger and Wettick, "Miranda in Pittsburgh—A Statistical Study," 29 *University of Pittsburgh Law Review* 1 (1967).

15 Fred Inbau, James Thompson, Claude Sowle, *Cases & Comments on Criminal Justice,* 3rd ed., vol. 2 (Mineola, N.Y.: The Foundation Press, 1968), pp. 695-698.

16 Medalie, Leitz and Alexander, "Custodial Police Interrogation in Our Nation's Capitol: The Attempt to Implement Miranda," 66 *Michigan Law Review* 1347 (1968).

17 Evelle J. Younger, "Results of a Survey Conducted in the District Attorney's Office of Los Angeles County Regarding the Effect of the *Miranda* Decision upon the Prosecution of Felony Cases," 5 *American Criminal Law Quarterly,* 5 (1966): 32.

[18] "Interrogations in New Haven: The Impact of *Miranda*," 76 *Yale Law Journal*, 76 (1967): 1519.

Chapter 9

[1] Francis C. Sullivan, "A Comparative Study of Problems in Criminal Procedure," 6 *St. Louis University Law Journal*, 380 (1961).

[2] Ibid.

[3] *Engle* v. *Chipman*, 51 Mich. 524 (1883).

[4] *United States* v. *Cox*, 342 F. 2d 167 (5th Cir., 1965).

[5] Jerome H. Skolnick, "Social Control In the Adversary System," 11 *Journal of Conflict Resolution*, 52 (1967).

Chapter 10

[1] J. Richard Roberts, "A Comparison of Non-Salaried Lawyers by Fields of Practice," 25 *Journal of the Missouri Bar*, 176 (1969).

[2] National Commission on Law Observance and Enforcement, *Criminal Justice Surveys Analysis* (Appendix To Report on Prosecutions) (Washington, D.C.: Government Printing Office, 1931), pp. 30-33.

[3] 287 U.S. 45, 53 S. Ct. 55, L. Ed. 158.

[4] *Hamilton* v. *Alabama*, 368 U.S. 52, 82 S. Ct. 157, 7 L. Ed. 2d 114 (1961).

[5] 316 U.S. 455, 62 S. Ct. 1252, 86 L. Ed. 1595.

[6] 372 U.S. 335, 83 S. Ct. 792, 9 L. Ed. 2d 799.

[7] Abraham S. Blumberg, *Criminal Justice* (Chicago: Quadrangle Books, 1967), pp. 93-115.

Chapter 11

[1] Arthur John Keeffe, "Current Legal Literature," 57 *American Bar Association Journal*, 89 (January, 1971).

[2] President's Commission on Law Enforcement and the Administration of Justice, *Task Force Report: The Courts*, pp. 37-38.

[3] Ibid.

Chapter 12

[1] The material presented in this chapter relates primarily to felony offenses, even though in some states certain types of misdemeanor cases may follow the same procedure.

Chapter 13

[1] Commenting on this practice the Wisconsin Supreme Court stated [*Jung* v. *State,* 32 Wis. 541, 145 N.W. 2d 684 (1966)]: "It is common knowledge there is a wide practice in the courts of this country of accepting pleas of guilty and giving lighter sentences than are generally given for the same crime after trial."

Chapter 14

[1] *Williams* v. *Florida,* 399 U.S. 78, 90 S. Ct. 1893, 26 L. Ed. 2d 446 (1970).

[2] *Swain* v. *Alabama,* 380 U.S. 202, 85 S. Ct. 824, 13 L. Ed. 2d 759 (1965).

[3] *Shapard* v. *State,* Okl. Cr., 437 P. 2d 565 (1967). The names of the parties have been changed.

[4] 22 Okla. Stat. 659.

Chapter 15

[1] *Illinois* v. *Allen,* 397 U.S. 337, 90 S. Ct. 1057, 25 L. Ed. 2d 353.

[2] *People* v. *Fuerback,* 66 Ill. App. 2d 452, 214 N.E. 2d 330 (1966).

[3] *Smith* v. *Illinois,* 390 U.S. 129, 88 S. Ct. 748, 19 L. Ed. 2d 956 (1968).

[4] *State* v. *Belk,* 268 N.C. 320, 150 S.E. 2d 481 (1966).

[5] *Berger* v. *United States,* 294 U.S. 78, 55 S. Ct. 629, 79 L. Ed. 1314 (1935).

Chapter 16

[1] Robert H. Scott, "Probation," in Marshall Houts *From Arrest to Release,* (Springfield: Charles C. Thomas Publisher, 1958), p. 115.

Chapter 17

[1] *Report of The President's Commission on Crime in the District of Columbia* (Washington, D.C.: Government Printing Office, 1966), p. 301.

[2] *Fay* v. *Noia,* 372 U.S. 391, 83 S. Ct. 822, 9 L. Ed. 2d 837 (1963).

Chapter 18

[1] President's Commission On Law Enforcement and the Administration of Justice, *Task Force Report: Corrections,* p. 63.

[2] "Criminals Should Be Cured, Not Caged," 6 *American Criminal Law Quarterly,* 133 (1968).

[3] *State* v. *Cannon,* 5 Storey 587, 190 A. 2d 514 (1963).

[4] *Jackson* v. *Bishop,* 4 Cr. L. 2243 (8 Cir., 1968).

[5] *Holt* v. *Shaver,* 309 F. Supp. 362, 6 Cf. L. 2380 (1969).

6 *Bryant* v. *Hendrick,* 7 Cr. L. 2463 (1970).

7 LEAA Newsletter, Vol. 1, No. 6 (March, 1971), p. 5.

8 President's Commission on Law Enforcement and Administration of Justice, *The Challenge Of Crime in a Free Society,* p. 159.

9 "President Nixon's Statement on the Crime Bill," 1 *Law Enforcement Assistance Administration Newsletter,* 3 (1971).

ANNOTATED BIBLIOGRAPHY

The following bibliography has been compiled for readers in further exploration of the ideas and concepts presented in this book. It is divided into four parts. Part I contains reference to the materials produced by the 1967 President's Commission on Law Enforcement and the Administration of Justice. Part II contains references to materials developed and published by the American Bar Association on Standards for Criminal Justice. Part III contains reference to a number of standard casebooks on criminal law and procedure. Part IV contains references relating to the specific chapters of this book.

PART I
THE PRESIDENT'S COMMISSION ON LAW ENFORCEMENT

In 1967 the President's Commission on Law Enforcement and Administration of Justice issued a series of reports. These reports are among the most significant criminal justice resource materials produced in the last thirty-five years. They may be obtained from the Government Printing Office, Washington, D.C., 20402.

Commission Report: The Challenge of Crime In A Free Society.

Task Force Report: Corrections.

Task Force Report: The Courts.

Task Force Report: Crime and Its Impact: An Assessment.

Task Force Report: Drunkenness.

Task Force Report: Juvenile Delinquency and Youth Crime.

Task Force Report: Narcotics and Drug Abuse.

Task Force Report: Organized Crime.

Task Force Report: The Police.

Task Force Report: Science and Technology.

Field Surveys I: Report on a Pilot Study in the District of Columbia on Victimization and Attitudes Toward Law Enforcement.

Field Surveys II: Criminal Victimization in the United States.

Field Surveys III: Studies in Crime and Law Enforcement in Major Metropolitan Areas (2 volumes).

Field Surveys IV: The Police and the Community (2 volumes).

Field Surveys V: National Survey of Police and Community Relations.

PART II
AMERICAN BAR ASSOCIATION PROJECT

The American Bar Association has conducted numerous studies and published a series of standards relating to the administration of criminal justice. Even though some of the standards are still in tentative form, there is little doubt that they will stimulate interest in improving the administration of criminal justice. Copies may be obtained from: Office of Criminal Justice Project, Institute of Judicial Administration, 40 Washington Square South, New York, New York, 10012.

Appellate Review of Sentences, 1967.

Criminal Appeals, 1969.

Discovery and Procedure Before Trial, 1969.

Electronic Surveillance, 1968.

Fair Trial and Free Press, 1966.

Joinder and Severance, 1967.

Pleas of Guilty, 1967.

Post Conviction Remedies, 1967.

Pretrial Release, 1968.

Probation, 1970.

The Prosecution Function and the Defense Function, 1970.

Providing Defense Services, 1967.

Sentencing Alternatives and Procedures, 1967.

Speedy Trial, 1967.

Trial by Jury, 1968.

The Urban Police Function, 1972.

PART III
CASEBOOKS ON CRIMINAL PROCEDURE

The following casebooks contain judicial cases, materials, and commentaries on the various processes of criminal justice examined in this book.

Hall, Livingston, Yale Kamisar, Wayne R. LaFave, and Jerold H. Israel. *Modern Criminal Procedure.* 3rd ed. St. Paul: West Publishing Co., 1969.

Hall, Livingston, and Sheldon Glueck. *Cases on Criminal Law and Its Enforcement.* 2nd ed. St. Paul: West Publishing Company, 1958.

Inbau, Fred E., James R. Thompson, and Claude R. Sowle. *Cases and Comments On Criminal Justice.* Vol. 2, 3rd ed. Mineola, N.Y.: The Foundation Press, Inc., 1968.

Perkins, Rollin M. *Cases and Materials on Criminal Law and Procedure.* 3rd ed. Mineola, N.Y.: The Foundation Press, Inc., 1966.

Sullivan, Francis C., Paul Hardin III, John Huston, Frank R. Lacy, Daniel E. Murray, and George W. Pugh. *Cases and Materials on the Administration of Criminal Justice.* 2nd ed. Mineola, N.Y.: The Foundation Press, Inc., 1969.

Weinreb, Lloyd L. *Criminal Law: Cases, Comments and Questions.* Mineola, N.Y.: The Foundation Press, Inc., 1969.

PART IV
REFERENCE SOURCES FOR SPECIFIC CHAPTERS

Chapter 1 — The Sources of Criminal Law

Clark, Grenville, ed. *The Future of the Common Law.* Cambridge: Harvard University Press, 1937.

This book contains a collection of papers presented at a Harvard Law School conference on common law directed by Roscoe Pound. The papers emphasize the principles underlying common law and their adaptability to changing social conditions.

Holmes, Oliver Wendell. *The Common Law.* Cambridge: Belknap Press of Harvard University Press, 1963.

This book contains a collection of the famous jurist's lectures. Lecture II has particular relevance to the person concerned with the philosophical development of the common law.

Howard, Charles G., and Robert S. Summers. *Law, Its Nature, Functions and Limits.* Englewood Cliffs, N.J.: Prentice-Hall, Inc., 1965.

This book portrays law, not as a series of regulations, but as man's primary means of social control. It concentrates on the operation of the legal system and emphasizes its significant functions.

Pound, Roscoe. *The Spirit of the Common Law.* Boston: Marshall Jones Co., 1921.

This book presents a philosophical analysis of the historical development of the common law.

Chapter 2 — The Effective Limits of Criminal Law

Allen, Francis A. *The Borderland of Criminal Justice.* Chicago: University of Chicago Press, 1964.

This book contains a group of essays with the central theme that criminal justice is not the proper vehicle for the administration of social services.

Clor, Harry M. *Obscenity and Public Morality.* Chicago: University of Chicago Press, 1969.

The author of this book develops the definition of obscenity and attempts to provide a systematic and reasoned argument for legal control.

Department of Health, Education and Welfare. *The Court and the Chronic Inebriate.* Washington, D.C.: Government Printing Office. 1965.

This monograph contains conference proceedings on the subject of drunkenness and alternative roles the courts may assume to aid in its alleviation.

Kendis, Joseph B., and Michael Laski. *The St. Louis Detoxification and Evaluation Center.* Washington, D.C.: Government Printing Office, 1970.

This book contains an analytical description of one of the most progressive programs dealing with drunkenness.

Morris, Norval, and Gordon Hawkins. *The Honest Politician's Guide to Crime Control.* Chicago: University of Chicago Press, 1970.

The basic premise of this book is that the criminal justice

system has been unwisely extended beyond its proper role into areas of private morality.

National Commission on Obscenity and Pornography. *Report.* Washington, D.C.: Government Printing Office, 1970.

This report is the most comprehensive study ever completed on obscenity and its effects. The report recommends the abolition of most obscenity laws.

Nimmer, Raymond T. *Two Million Unnecessary Arrests.* Chicago: American Bar Foundation, 1971.

This publication reports on a study of the problem of public drunkenness and the means of removing it from the criminal process.

Packer, Herbert L. *The Limits of the Criminal Sanction.* Stanford: Stanford University Press, 1968.

One of the most scholarly books realistically facing the question of the limitations of criminal law, both philosophically and practically.

Schur, Edwin M. *Crimes Without Victims: Deviant Behavior and Public Policy.* Englewood Cliffs, N.J.: Prentice-Hall, Inc., 1965.

This book examines abortion, homosexuality, and drug addiction, and raises fundamental questions about defining criminal conduct, unenforcibility of laws, and the secondary pathology created by such laws.

Chapter 3 — The Establishment and Control of Police Agencies

Germann, A. C., Frank Day, and Robert Gallati. *Introduction to Law Enforcement and Criminal Justice.* Springfield: Charles C. Thomas Publishers, 1972.

For a listing of the various federal law enforcement agencies and a description of their functions see pages 143-155.

Smith, Bruce. *Police Systems in the United States.* 2nd rev. ed. New York: Harper & Row, Publishers, 1960.

This book examines the origin and extension of police agencies and the numerous political problems they encounter.

The following are classic texts relating to the American police system and police administration:

Fuld, Leonard Felix. *Police Administration.* New York: G. P. Putnam's Sons, 1909.

Leonard, V. A. *Police Organization and Management.* 2nd ed. Brooklyn: The Foundation Press, Inc., 1964.

Vollmer, August. *The Police and Modern Society.* College Park: McGrath Publishing Co., 1970. [Reprint of the 1936 Edition.]

Wilson, O. W. *Police Administration.* 2nd ed. New York: McGraw-Hill Book Co., 1963.

Chapter 4 — The Authority to Arrest

Creamer, J. Shane. *The Law of Arrest, Search and Seizure.* Philadelphia: W. B. Saunders Company, 1968.

This book provides practical insight into the major areas of arrest law affected by recent Supreme Court decisions.

LaFave, Wayne R. *Arrest: The Decision to Take a Suspect Into Custody,* Boston: Little, Brown & Co., 1965.

A scholarly work of exceptional merit, this book examines current practices in order to discover and define problems relating to the arrest decision. Each issue relating to the arrest decision is examined.

Also see the relevant sections of the books listed in Part III of this bibliography.

Chapter 5 — The Discretionary Use and Abuse of the Arrest Power

Chevigny, Paul. *Police Power: Police Abuses in New York City.* New York: Pantheon Books, Inc., 1969.

The author examines patterns of police abuse and alleges that false arrest is a common police response to encounters with difficult persons. He then examines the difficulty that one falsely arrested has in proving his innocence.

Cray, Ed. *The Big Blue Line: An Urgent Report on Police Powers vs. Human Rights, Examining Brutality in the Streets, Malpractice in the Station House, Crisis in the Courts.* New York: Coward McCann and Geoghegan, Inc., 1967.

The title of this book, written by the director of publications for the American Civil Liberties Union of Southern California, adequately describes its contents.

Davis, Kenneth Culp. *Discretionary Justice: A Preliminary Inquiry.* Baton Rouge: Louisiana State University Press, 1969.

In this very scholarly work, the author examines the amount of discretion in the criminal justice system and advances concrete proposals for reforming the system.

Goldstein, Herman. "Full Enforcement Versus Police Discretion Not to Invoke the Criminal Process" in *Police and Community Relations: A Sourcebook.* A. F. Brandstatter and Louis Radelet, eds. Beverly Hills: Glencoe Press, 1968.

Goldstein, Herman. "Police Discretion: The Ideal Versus the Real" in *The Ambivalent Force: Prospectives on the Police.* Arthur Neiderhoffer and Abraham Blumberg, eds. Waltham, Mass.: Ginn & Co., 1970.

In these two essays Goldstein recognizes the vast amount of discretion exercised by police and recommends proper methods of channelling this discretion.

Heusseustamm, F. K. "Bumper Stickers and the Cops." *Transaction,* February, 1971.

The article reports on a sociological study establishing the correlation between bumper stickers on automobiles and the drivers' receipt of traffic violation citations.

LaFave, Wayne R. *Arrest: The Decision to Take a Suspect into Custody*. Boston: Little, Brown & Co., 1965.

This book examines current use of discretion and attempts to isolate the many factors which affect the way an officer exercises it.

Niederhoffer, Arthur. *Behind the Shield: The Police in Urban Society.* Garden City: Doubleday & Co., Inc., 1967.

This book examines, among other things, the policeman's responsibility to decide if and how the law shall be applied and the various factors affecting that decision.

Chapter 6 — Detention Short of Arrest

Bristow, Allen P. *Field Interrogation.* 2nd ed. Springfield: Charles C. Thomas, Publisher, 1964.

This book examines the methodologies and the effectiveness of field interrogation techniques.

Tiffany, Lawrence P., Donald M. McIntyre, Jr., and Daniel L. Rotenberg. *Detection of Crime: Stopping and Questioning, Search and Seizure, Encouragement and Entrapment.* Boston: Little, Brown & Co., 1967.

This scholarly book details the problems and conflicts raised by police detection methods and makes recommendations for their solution. Part I of the book deals directly with the problem of stopping and questioning.

Also see the relevant sections of the books listed in Part III of this bibliography.

Chapter 7 — Searches

Department of Justice. *Handbook on the Law of Search and Seizure.* Washington, D.C.: Government Printing Office (constantly updated).

This handbook is designed to provide law enforcement officers with a readily available source of information concerning the current status of the law of search and seizure.

Nedrud, Duane R. *The Supreme Court and the Law of Criminal Investigation.* Chicago: Laurel Editions of Dell Publishing Co., Inc., 1968.

A handbook containing case excerpts and analyses which provide concise guidelines for arrest, search, and seizure cases.

Tiffany, Lawrence P., Donald M. McIntyre, Jr., and Daniel L. Rotenberg. *Detection of Crime: Stopping and Questioning, Search and Seizure, Encouragement and Entrapment.* Boston: Little, Brown & Co., 1967.

Part II of this book presents a scholarly study of the current practices of officers in search and seizure cases.

Also see the relevant sections of the books listed in Part III of this bibliography.

Chapter 8 — Interrogating the Accused

Inbau, Fred E., and John E. Reid, *Criminal Interrogation and Confessions.* 2nd ed., Baltimore: Williams & Wilkins, 1967.

This book is the classic text on tactics and techniques utilized in criminal investigation and interrogation, with an analysis of the law of confession. For an interesting comparison prior to *Escobedo-Miranda,* see the authors' first edition published in 1962 and Part II of Inbau's *Lie Detection and Criminal Interrogation,* 1st ed., 1942; 2nd ed., 1948; and 3rd ed. with Reid, 1953.

Other general texts relating the general concepts and methods of interrogation:

Arther, Richard O., and Rudolph R. Caputo, *Interrogation for Investigators.* New York: William C. Copp and Associates, 1959.

Aubrey, Arthur S., Jr. *The Officer in the Small Department.* Springfield: Charles C. Thomas, Publisher, 1961. (Chapter 17: "Interviews and Interrogations".)

Fitzgerald, Maurice J. *Handbook of Criminal Investigation.* New York: Arco Publishing Company, Inc., 1951. (Chapter VI: "Interrogation Techniques".)

Mulbar, Harold. *Interrogation.* Springfield: Charles C. Thomas, Publisher, 1951.

O'Hara, Charles E. *Fundamentals of Criminal Investigation.* 2nd ed., Springfield: Charles C. Thomas, Publisher, 1970. (Chapter 9: "Interrogations".)

Vanderbosch, Charles G. *Criminal Investigation.* Washington, D.C.: International Assn. of Chiefs of Police, 1968. (Chapter XV: "Democratic Guidelines of Interrogation".)

Weston, Paul B., and Kenneth M. Wells. *Criminal Investigation: Basic Perspectives.* Englewood Cliffs, N.J.: Prentice-Hall, Inc. 1970. (Chapter Twelve: "Interrogation".)

Also see the relevant sections of the books listed in Part III of this bibliography.

Chapter 9 — Prosecution

Bettman, Alfred. *Prosecution.* Cleveland: The Cleveland Foundation, 1921.

This is a report of the 1921 study of the administration of criminal justice in Cleveland. It gives significant insight into the prosecutor's function.

Botein, Bernard. *The Prosecutor.* New York: Simon & Schuster, Inc., 1956.

This *novel* describes the internal struggles within a prosecutor's organization and the use and abuse of discretion. Written by an eminent jurist, one suspects that this book contains more fact than fancy.

Miller, Frank W. *Prosecution: The Decision to Charge a Suspect with a Crime.* Boston: Little, Brown & Co., 1969.

This book examines the many factors which compromise the decision to charge, concentrating on the prosecutor's role.

Moley, Raymond. *Politics and Criminal Prosecution.* New York: G. P. Putnam's Sons, 1929.

Pages 95 through 126 of this book contain an excellent historical review of the medieval predecessors of the prosecutor and the development of his office.

The following biographies and autobiographies concerning the prosecutor's functions are both enlightening and enjoyable reading.

Frank, Martin M. *Diary of a D.A.* New York: Holt, Rinehart & Winston, 1960.

Mills, James. *The Prosecutor.* New York: Farrar, Straus, and Giroux, Inc., 1969.

Traver, Robert. *Small Town D.A.* New York: E. P. Dutton and Co., Inc., 1954.

Traver, Robert. *Trouble-Shooter: The Story of a Northwoods Prosecutor.* New York: Viking Press, Inc., 1943.

Also see the relevant sections of the materials contained in Parts I, II, and III of this bibliography.

Chapter 10 — The Defense Attorney

Blumberg, Abraham H. *Criminal Justice.* Chicago: Quadrangle Books, Inc., 1967.

Chapter 5 of this book portrays the defense attorney as an "agent-mediator" and indicates that he is as much a part of the bureaucratic system as any other criminal justice functionary. As such, Blumberg feels that the defense attorney is more interested in the efficiency of the system than in preserving the defendant's rights.

Day, Frank D. *Criminal Law and Society*. Springfield: Charles C. Thomas, Publisher, 1964.

Chapter 7 of this book indicts lawyers and law schools for their lack of interest in the criminal law and advocates increased emphasis in this area.

Lewis, Anthony. *Gideon's Trumpet*. New York; Random House, Inc., 1964.

This book provides an extremely detailed analysis of the events leading to the United States Supreme Court decision in *Gideon v. Wainwright.*

The following biographical and autobiographical materials relating to defense attorneys and their cases are recommended for additional insight into the defense attorney's methods and strategies.

Bailey, F. Lee. *The Defense Never Rests*. New York: Stein & Day, 1971.

Belli, Melvin M. *Dallas Justice: The Real Story of Jack Ruby and His Trial.* New York: David McKay Co., Inc., 1964.

Dorman, Michael. *King of the Courtroom: Percy Foreman for the Defense.* New York: Delacorte Press, 1969.

Fowler, Gene. *The Great Mouthpiece: A Life Story of William J. Fallon.* New York: Crown Publishers, Inc., 1931.

Frank, Gerald. *The Boston Strangler*. New York: New American Library, Inc., 1966. [F. Lee Bailey]

Giesler, Jerry. *Hollywood Lawyer: The Jerry Giesler Story*. New York: Simon & Schuster, 1960.

Holmes, Paul. *Retrial: Murder and Doctor Sam Sheppard.* New York: Bantam Books, Inc., 1966. [F. Lee Bailey]

Holmes, Paul. *The Trials of Dr. Coppolina.* New York: New American Library, Inc., 1967. [F. Lee Bailey]

House, Brant, ed. *Great Trials of Famous Lawyers.* New York: Ace Books, 1962. [Darrow, Davis, Fallon, Hays, Leibowitz, Rogers, Steuer and Vanderveer]

Newsweek Magazine, "Bailey for the Defense." April 17, 1967, pp. 35-43.

Rovere, Richard H. *Howe and Hummel: Criminal Lawyers,* New York: Farrar, Straus, and Giroux, Inc., 1947.

Stone, Irving. *Clarence Darrow for the Defense.* New York: Doubleday & Co., Inc., 1941.

Whitten, Les. *F. Lee Bailey.* New York: The Avon Books, 1971.

Chapter 11 — Preliminary Proceedings

See the American Bar Association, *Pretrial Release* cited in Part II and relevant section of the other materials contained in Parts I, II, and III of this bibliography.

Chapter 12 — Preliminary Proceedings in the Trial Court

See the American Bar Association, *Discovery and Procedure Before Trial,* cited in Part II, and relevant sections of the other materials contained in Parts I, II, and III of this bibliography.

Chapter 13 — Conviction Without Trial: The Guilty Plea

Newman, Donald J. *Conviction: The Determination of Guilt or Innocence Without Trial.* Boston: Little, Brown & Co., 1966.

This book analyzes the various components of nontrial adjudication and describes the various practices utilized by prosecutors and judges. It concentrates on the issues of accepting guilty pleas, the propriety of plea bargaining, and the role of defense counsel.

Skolnick, Jerome H. *Justice Without Trial.* New York: John Wiley & Sons, Inc., 1966.

This book vividly illustrates that most criminal cases reach their dispositions on the street, in the station house, in the prosecutor's office, or the judge's chambers. It shows criminal justice as a bureaucratic or administrative system rather than an adversary system.

See also the American Bar Association, *Pleas of Guilty,* cited in Part II, and relevant sections of the other materials contained in Parts I, II, and III of this bibliography.

Chapter 14 — The Trial Jury and Its Selection

Kalven, Harry, Jr., and Hans Zeisel. *The American Jury.* Boston: Little, Brown & Co., 1966.

This book is a fascinating pioneer effort into the decision-making processes of criminal case juries. Over 3,500 jury cases from throughout the United States are analyzed and the various factors influencing the decisions are detailed.

Also see the relevant materials contained in Parts II and III of this bibliography.

Chapter 15 — The Trial

See American Bar Association, *Trial By Jury,* cited in Part II, and the relevant sections of materials contained in Part III.

Chapter 16 — The Sentencing Decision

Dawson, Richard O. *Sentencing: The Decision as to Type, Length and Conditions of Sentence.* Boston: Little, Brown & Co., 1969.

This book analyzes the methods utilized in obtaining presentencing information; the probation system and the decision to grant or deny probation; the general conditions of probation; the probationer's supervision; revocation actions; and determination of length of incarceration.

Also see American Bar Association, *Sentencing Alternatives and Procedures* and *Probation,* cited in Part II, and the relevant sections of the materials contained in Parts I and III of this bibliography.

Chapter 17 — Appeals and Postconviction Reviews

See American Bar Association, *Criminal Appeals* and *Post Conviction Remedies,* cited in Part II, and relevant sections of materials contained in Part III of this bibliography.

Chapter 18 — Incarceration and Release

The following general texts will provide the reader opportunity for additional exploration of the correctional field.

Carter, Robert M., and Leslie T. Wilkins. *Probation and Parole: Selected Readings.* New York: John Wiley & Sons, Inc., 1970.

Cressey, Donald R., and David A. Ward. *Delinquency, Crime, and Social Process.* New York: Harper & Row, Publishers, 1969.

Johnson, Elmer Hubert. *Crime, Correction and Society.* Homewood, Illinois: Dorsey Press, Inc., 1968.

Johnston, Norman, Leonard Savitz, and Marvin E. Wolfgang, eds. *The Sociology of Punishment and Correction.* 2nd ed. New York: John Wiley & Sons, Inc., 1970.

Tappan, Paul W. *Crime, Justice and Correction.* New York: McGraw-Hill Book Co., Inc., 1960.

Wilkins, Leslie T. *Evaluation of Penal Measures.* New York: Random House, Inc., 1969.

Also see President's Commission, *Task Force Report: Corrections,* cited in Part I of this bibliography.

Chapter 19 — Reconciling Efficiency and Legality

The following books provide insight into the issue of efficiency versus legality.

Barth, Alan. *The Price of Liberty.* New York: Viking Press, Inc., 1961.

Chevigny, Paul. *Police Power: Police Abuses In New York City.* New York: Pantheon Books, Inc., 1969.

Clark, Ramsey. *Crime in America.* New York: Simon & Schuster, 1970.

Cray, Ed. *The Big Blue Line: Police Power vs. Human Rights.* New York: Coward-McCann and Geoghegan, Inc., 1968.

President's Commission on Campus Unrest. *Campus Unrest.* Washington, D.C.: Government Printing Office, 1970.

Walker, Daniel. *Rights In Conflict: The Violent Confrontation of Demonstrators and Police in the Parks and Streets of Chicago During the Week of the Democratic National Convention.* New York: E. P. Dutton & Co., Inc., 1968.

The following are thought-provoking *novels* on repressive systems of social control.

Bradbury, Ray. *Fahrenheit 451.* New York: Ballantine Books, Inc., 1953.

Golding, William. *Lord of the Flies.* New York: G. P. Putnam's Sons, 1954.

Huxley, Aldous. *Brave New World.* New York: Harper and Brothers, 1932. [Also see Huxley's essay *Brave New World Revisited.* New York: Harper & Row, Publishers, 1958.]

Levin, Ira. *This Perfect Day.* New York: Random House, Inc., 1970.

Orwell, George. *Nineteen Eighty-Four.* New York: New American Library, Inc., 1949.